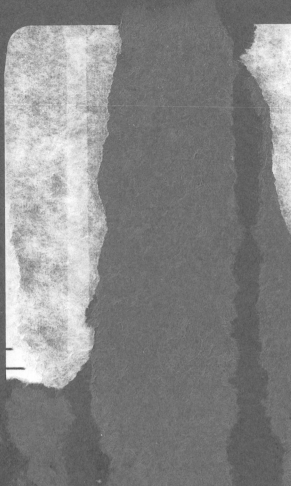

COINY PUBLISHING CO., INC.

Phone 317 462-7758
Email TEQW@aol.com

P.O.BOX 585
GREENFIELD, INDIANA 46140

RE: Gift of a Hoosier Deutsch Folklore piece set in the late Nineteenth Century: **The Wild Bull of Blue River**, Daniel Matthew Williams.

Maam or Sir:

We forward for your library a gift of a work of American Folk Literature. The gift is made to library resources as directed out of the stock of the book of the provider in memory of his brother, the author.

Sincerely,

Coiny Pub

The Wild Bull of Blue River

A HOOSIER CHRISTMAS TALE

by

DANIEL MATTHEW WILLIAMS

COINY PUBLISHING CO.
P.O. Box 585,
Greenfield, IN 46140
317-462-7758

❄

Library Of Congress Catalog
Card Number 95-92305

Williams, Daniel M. (1949, Deceased)

ISBN 1-887495-00-2

1. Fiction, American. 2. Folklore Tales, American. 3.(Nt)
Folklore Tales, Indiana.

Printed In The United States Of America

TABLE OF CONTENTS

❋

The Wild Bull

If you had been living in the Central Indiana of the 1890s, you would have known about the Wild Bull of Blue River. Everybody did. He was as much a topic of conversation as the discovery of natural gas and the mad rush of Gas Boom industries to Greenfield, Indiana, and its sister cities and towns in the heartland of the Hoosier Deutsch. The area rode on a dome of the nauseous gold. But what good is gold if you can't live to spend it?

The Wild Bull was a terrible creature, a bull that no farmer claimed and no one could seem to kill that roamed the Blue River Valley. At night you could sense him. The bull was an assassin on the loose in the night.

Just when you wanted to go sit outside and enjoy the cooling night air after a hot summer day, you would hear the bull's thrashings about in the woods or fields. You would fear anger or raw power was on the loose and you would want to go inside. Death, wearing steely sharp horns, might come into your farmyard. It was unsettling to say the least, living near a murdering animal unfettered. The Hoosier Deutsch farmkids would go to bed with the prayer, "God, keep me from bein' hornt."

There wasn't any question what the Wild Bull looked like. Lots of folks had seen him with his pure Hereford horns thick and reaching a killing point so sharp that they could cut and tear through a barn door or destroy with a swoop any wire mesh fence that a farmer might put up in the vain hope of keeping him out.

Once you saw the Wild Bull's narrow set eyes, highlighted by his white face, you would never forget their stare. It was fearless, powerful and confident. It demanded respect and obedience. One avoided that stare at all costs much as would a prisoner on death row wish to avoid the look of an executioner because to see him would be to know you were in ultimate peril and that the end was near.

These beady eyes were set on a 2,000 pound red frame filled out in muscle and grit, red except for the white underside, breast, switch, crest, and below the knees and hocks. One could not wrestle with that. If such a bulk came at you with the force and intention of knocking you over, you had best get out of the way. One does not stand in a bowling alley lane when a bowling ball is directed at the pins. You could think of the Wild Bull as a bowling ball when it had in mind to drive through some place. A cracking and shattering might result.

And yet to the workforce of common laborers at the Weston Paper Manufacturing Company on the east end of Greenfield, one of the many factories that moved to Greenfield for free gas and free land, there were other matters far more pressing.

2

A Mill Girl Named Lamb

Seeing the vast factory there to the East of Greenfield on the Morristown Pike, rising high on the hill east of Brandywine Creek, you would never imagine a girl working inside whose looks were like magic. But it was so. Lamb Hackleman, a little Deutsch girl fresh from the farmlands of the Blue River Valley, not only worked there but almost could have called the place her home. At 18, she was vigorous and sharp-eyed, even if she did become tired easily after the first few hours. The mill girls were expected to work summer and winter hours with the start time of each at ten minutes to sunrise each day. Lamb did not mind. It was better to wake up to work rather than to live a life of loneliness.

Lamb was glad to have employment. How could she have supported herself otherwise? She could not return to the farm home where she had grown up down in Blue River Township of the county, much closer to the vein of the Blue River itself. No, she had to leave the lands where her girlish youth had been lived.

And she had become just one of the girls keeping the Greenfield Paper Mill going. Oh, there were men working there as well - it was not just a female enterprise. Lamb knew that the eyes of some of these men turned to her, but she could never return the look. She could never love another man after having known the love she had once experienced. She was at the mill for the wages. Lamb and her component who operated the cooking digesters of the straw were an essential part of the plant's operation.

What a jewel this factory was in the crown of Greenfield during the Gas Boom days of the wildly extravagant 1890's. The mill was the largest straw wrapping paper mill in the world! The Green-field Board of Trade, a group of the town's most prominent bankers, lawyers, and merchants, had courted the owners of the Ohio-based Weston Paper Manufacturing Company like lovers to get them to move their factory location to Greenfield. The offer of free natural gas had been the major draw. Also the site was a benefit. Huge water demands were met by diverting water from the artesian wells on the east bank of the Brandywine and the "used" water after the straw was cooked could be dumped into Brandywine Creek - and yes, the company promised the water would not pollute the mumbling little creek with its white barked sycamores setting exclamation points of beauty along its meanders.

Lamb had been employed there almost from its opening in the early fall of 1892. The mill was built in record time. The owner's agent, Mr. Rock, insisted it be completed in time for the purchasing agents to fan out over the farm lands to make their buys of straw from a last autumn cutting. The investors insisted the plant be run from a profit from its very start and paper be produced beginning immediately. Those early days had flown by and now was the time when the mill was gearing up for the first spring cutting of straw from the surrounding farms of Hancock County, purchased in huge lots.

Lamb would work at this mill no matter what and there were drawbacks. The air around the mill always seemed so vaporous and noxious. The cooks of the straw could only partially be at blame because the soda steam would arise and cloud the sky on days when the air refused to rise or was forced down by colder fronts moving over the Hoosier lands. But it was more than that. Almost everything that touched the mill seemed to be fumy and perturbing to the air - the heating plants, the smoke stacks on every building, and even the steam locomotives coming to and from the mill on the iron rails. Even they belched out burning clouds of discharge. The effect of all this ethereality was that the contours and lines of the buildings seemed blurred and less substantial than they really were. Not until one left the premises did the air resume its freshness and wholesomeness.

Here would come the farmers into town on the east side on the newly graveled National Road, only recently turned back into a public thoroughfare from its former status as a failed turnpike. Behind the farmers, mounted on their wagon benches in wagons, pulled by teams of horses, mostly stout dour-faced Hoosier Deutschmen, would be the loads of straw on wagons. The straw would be deposited in the level courtyard of the huge factory up the road near the central one story "cooking" building with its huge stack shooting up into the air 100 feet high.

Such a farmer might quickly make his sale and leave the premises amazed at the extent of the factory itself for the digester building where the straw would be cooked was only one of the many buildings at the place. Surrounding the digester edifice, like an "L," was a low-strung building over 100 feet wide. At the south end of the L, the building was elongated at the point where it fronted the Panhandle Railroad. The elongation consisted of shipping facilities, actually two additional buildings, one on each side of the "L" extension. On the other side of the railroad spur was another storage building too. To the north of the huge grounds was the final building and its biggest, a three story monstrous brick building that was actually so large its foundation was built into the slope of the hill on which the rest of the factory was located, so that its first level was at the foot of the factory hill which came to be known as Strawboard Hill.

Such a factory would dwarf any person and render him or her almost insignificant one would think. But not so. In fact the bustle of the working folk emphasized it all. And the place was not one of brick but of busy sounds. Here was the hum of the press, the hiss of the digesters, the grind of the conveyer belts, the roar of the generators producing the factory's electricity, here the thud of the rolls of paper at the docks, there the shrill from the boiler, the neigh of the factory teams of horses, and the screech from the locking of the railroad boxcars' wheels along the tracks.

Lamb Hackleman would earn her livelihood in this place, hardly enough to get by on because the wages were notoriously low, but her heart was elsewhere. There wasn't a moment, in fact, when her thoughts did not fly from the paper mill where she worked back to the hovel across the street, in the Gas Boom workers' camp called Oklahoma, where a little child of her love would be awaiting her return no matter what the hour, and no matter how short would be the time they could have together.

And her hours at the paper mill were not lonely anyway because they were shared with her memory of a man far away with whom she had shared the sunnier days of her life.

And if there had been nothing else gained from her love, at least she had the pleasant recollection of the stolen days with her beloved in the wilds of the crick country of Blue River. She had known love, perhaps something that few ever can truly feel. She had got to know the man so very well that she would be able to love him forever. It would be no regret that she could never again return to the place, the lair of the Wild Bull, for she had known a man so fine and good that those days would ever be alive in her memory to comfort her against the buffeting of these days of poverty and hard labor.

She was so glad she had not known how it would end, this love they had shared, or she might not have had the courage to fall so deeply in love. But she had been there and having been there knew that her love was a star to guide her through her days and guide her across every sea of trouble.

3

A Day In The Mill

You could tell it was a Hoosier April even from the inside of the paper mill where the teenaged farm girl, Lamb Hackleman, worked. And what a beautiful afternoon it must have been outside, too! The air was much fuller than usual, bounteously energizing and warming and so much as tantalizingly talking to you with invitations to join in the joy of the land now so green, so new, and so happy that you were sharing in it all.

There would yet be time, when the factory closed, for Lamb to see it and feel it - this outside Hoosier land in spring renewal.

But for now there were still the last jobs of the afternoon "cook" to be done. Lamb's work was there, where the cooking proceeded, in the digester building where straw was reduced down to its fibers. Paper is, of course, just that, fibers that are rearranged from pulps of various kinds to form paper. The Greenfield mill used straw as the source of fiber rather than the more common wood or linen fibers from rags, or the esparto often utilized in Europe. Using straw for its fibers in papermaking was an experiment and a gamble. The Greenfield mill was America's first major throw of the dice.

Logically, straw should have worked as a source of paper fibers. Our newspapers of today should be printed on straw fibers. That they are not is a great shame since strawfields are a far more easily renewable natural resource than woodlands and straw would have made a wonderful crop for Hoosier agriculture. Instead foresters in the West now remove whole sweeps of forest to harvest trees and to supply current paper fiber needs. In the 1890s there was great expectation that the Greenfield paper mill would establish Indiana as a major producer of paper products from straw.

Lamb's work was with this straw. She and her crew of young girls would draw out its precious fibers, a necessary process before the cook could be sent on into other work locations. After the processing at the digester, the cook would be sent to the bleaching area and then, much transformed, into the paper machine located in the huge building built into the foot of the hill.

The work always seemed so exhausting in the afternoon. Lamb was not able to find nearly so much energy in the afternoons as in the mornings. The employment hours were determined by the hours of daylight rather than a clock. Dawn determined when the girls were expected to be at work and the dusk tolled their labors. The plant owners benevolently provided, however, that the plant should cease its operations in sufficient time for the girls to have light of day for a safe return to their homes.

There seemed no letting up - not even a little - from the time the yardmen delivered the straw for the first day's cook, dumping it in mountainous piles for the girl's sorting. Here would come a load. There would be a snorting of the yard horses, as they rested, while the sweating young yardmen, their arms muscled and bodies tense, forked off the grassy raw materials for a new batch. How taunting came the friendly verbal interchanges between the men and the girls! Then Lamb and the other girls would set to their tasks of separating the straw into small bunches for feeding into the top of the digester. The digester was a hungry machine which might be thought of as a large oblong kettle stood on end with a cone shaped bottom. The feeding was done from the top of the digester as with a kettle. After this feeding the top of the digester, now filled with separated straw, was bolted down with swing bolts, and the girls would await their new tasks of mopping the floors of the spill out of the black liquor from the digester. This was the most nauseating of the work because the spill contained the caustic soda within the tank that did the breaking down of the straw into its fibers. The digester was, after all, only riveted iron plates, and the steam injected into the digester, the heat to speed the cook, also meant that some of the soda liquor was squeezed out, leaking in constant little puddles that made breathing hard. The cook ordinarily took about three hours, but depended somewhat on the temperature inside the digester. The heat within the digester was so difficult to control! It had to be checked every so often by the foreman of the crew, Gustavus Crider. If too cool, Mr. Crider would have to adjust the steam valve to build up heat and its new pressure would cause the acid to bead and flow outside the tank all over again giving Lamb and the other mill girls further mopping to do.

The mopping was merely mechanical labor, even if it could be exhausting. Lamb didn't mind it, thinking of the digester as merely a person like herself sweating with its task. It was merely a metal child needing her maternal care.

Her more difficult jobs came at the ends of the cook. Then the fibers were blown out of the digester tank through opening its valve at the bottom and the cook escaped the tank through a pipe which routed the fibrous mess into a separator. Here the water of the clear Brandywine Creek replaced the caustic soda bath called its "black liquor." Men were given the work at the separator. The factory could be run at a profit only if the soda could be re-used and the process of distilling it out of the black liquor for re-use was placed in their masculine hands.

Lamb and the other country girls brought in to the factory from the farms were given the clean up of the digester - there was always some acidic mess inside because the solution never fully decomposed the straw - and its perforated plates, valves and piping inlets, and the steam circulating pump and equipment.

You might have thought that Lamb would have appeared as a wreck by the later afternoons at the factory or by the end of the day, but not so. Lamb Hackleman was a beautiful teenage girl whose grace could not be beaten down after working the daylight hours of the day. Her attractiveness radiated whether she was engaged in heavy factory labor or not. She would have appeared magical under any circumstance. Youth renewed her as well as her attributes which, like the fresh dawn, constantly reappear no matter how turbulent had been the weather of the prior day.

There was nothing heroic in her countenance. She was not an Amazon or even a large girl. In fact her height was somewhat

shorter than the usual. She was only a shadow over 5 feet. But she
would be someone with whom every young man in the place would
wildly imagine that he should like to spend time. She was beautiful
in softness so incongruent with the harshness of the labor she did.
The wisps of the light brown hair, turned blonder in their distraction from the rest, were always gently redone into their fixture with
combs after being undone during the strawing, mopping and cleaning. And she took care, in consonance with her Deutsch upbring-
ing, to always be clean as well as industrious. Her ankle length skirt
should never be awry or spotted long with the nasty black liquor
spotting. No matter how dark the inside of the brick digester or
how caustic its occasional atmosphere, never would Lamb's eyes
lose their glimmer and attraction. Nor would any shadow of any of
the redundant blaring electric lights cause a shadow to rest upon
her cheek for her skin was fair and with the irrepressibleness of late
adolescent blooming.

Only her hands gave her away as being a worker of the most
common labor. They had by now, after the first months, been
worked into callouses so that they were almost leathery. They had
been exposed too often to the handling of broom and mop and the
rubs and tiny gauging of a thousand blades of straw to escape this
result. Her hands revealed that Lamb Hackleman was no longer a
pampered child of the large Hoosier Deutsch farm of her ancestry.
Instead she had become a worker of the most strenuous labor.

The calloused and leathery hands also gave her the greatest
distress of her life for these were the hands which she would have
had as soft as the clouds to pick up the child of her love, to reach
for and caress this babe for whom she worked and breathed, now
awaiting her in the little hovel in Oklahoma, the Greenfield Gas
Boom workers' camp across the National Road from the paper mill
where she would soon escape following this day's, as the last's,
work.

Oklahoma was the name of the place where Lamb Hackleman
lived. For the most part Oklahoma would appear to a casual
observer as a crowded jumble of bantam boxlike wooden resi-
dences built close to the ground, in simple proportions and very

close together, with quaintly sized windows framed without regard to standard sizes. Sunlight could not reach the widths between most houses. The windows were covered not with standard sizes of glass but of greased paper for the most part, glass being a luxury few could afford here. Diminutive tar paper porches fronted several of the front doors. Small stretches of fencing or boundary markings in stone could be seen or an occasional garden. The folk of the place lounged in the front yards or on the small porches on simple chairs or boxes or steps and on warm evenings such as this one greeted with a wave those who passed by. Everyone knew each other by appearance but few knew names to go with the faces. Everyone also tried to know everyone else's business, a fact much to the chagrin of most, because everyone in Oklahoma had some secret characterization much regretted.

Few trees provided shelter here. The site of the encampment or "town" had once been oak and poplar forest but that was long ago. Oklahoma had been mostly cleared field before the industrialists of the town's Board of Trade had purchased it and subdivided it into the tiny tracts it was now for workers to inhabit. The lilliputian lots reflected the industrialists' belief that their workers should have something they could afford. Whatever trees left when the acreage was purchased had quickly been cleared for firewood. There were few shrubs but those that did dot the place were profuse and wildly extravagant with color as comes from the burning orange of the firebush or the prissy white streams of bridal wreath.

Oklahoma was obviously a place of the poor and a residential accident where no occupant would have easy resources to dream.

4

An Escape Into The Country

The day had been long, and the night was not far off when Lamb was permitted to leave her work at the Greenfield Paper Mill on Morristown Pike. It was a Saturday, late in the day, and the weekend beckoned. Sunday was the only day off and provided the only hours when the mill hands did not work. Relief would soon be within her grasp. She must rush to hold her child. And she would. Her child was the secret of her life and the air of her every breath.

Lamb crossed the roughly graveled National Road to reach the Gas Boom workers' camp called Oklahoma where she lived and where the little boy waited whose love and need of her was enough to carry her through the days and sustain her nightly dreads.

Why the rush? Ask Lamb Hackleman's heart if it could slow its flutter. It could not. It spirited her in its own hurry. She was going to the presence of her little boy. Lamb loved the child with a love that had a desperate character. Soon enough would come the time when the dark secret of her life would come out and the child would look upon Lamb, his mother, differently. Soon enough would come the day when the boy would see in his mother's eyes a woman of shame. But now-she must catch them while she could - there would be moments before that horrible time inevitably approaching. Now the mother and child could know and love each other as innocents deliriously happy that they had each other. And for the present Lamb's naive child could look into her eyes and not see the disrepute seen by the rest of the world.

Lamb rushed down a mud-packed street of Oklahoma, a place overcrowding with more and more Gas Boom transients come to

Indiana - and Greenfield - in search of the new jobs in industrial plants fueled by free natural gas on sites of free land. Every day seemed more a frenzy of the Hoosier town's Gas Boom, and every day seemed to leave Oklahoma in worse condition than before.

The home she would seek was on the third parallel street north of the National Road and one characterized by having porches front and back. This house was next to a more recent one temporarily built of poles and dubbed with spring mud. Lamb's dwelling was also taller than most, actually a small high gabled house built on the model of the frontier log home, with a second floor sleeping attic accessible by ladder. Downstairs was a single room. Lamb's quarters were a corner of this lower room.

Lamb was not the owner of this residence. The Ferrees were in fact the owner of the property. Mr. Ferree, the man of the house, wisely invested the small sum necessary for its pinch of land before his feet had been smashed in an industrial accident at the Conklin Iron Works, another Gas Boom industry nearby. Now it was he who cared for Lamb's child most during the days, accepting as rent and child care Lamb's slight earnings from the Weston Paper Manufacturing Co. Mrs. Ferree was a busy woman, too busy with the care of her own business to care much for Lamb's babe. She took in laundry from the Greenfield residents of the town proper.

The home was graced with a steeply angled porch covered by wood shingles across the front and another across the back which opened into a tiny garden where every vegetable that Mr. Ferree could cram into its well tended rows was cultivated. Soon would come a flood of fresh vegetables to the impoverished family.

Now as Lamb raced the last steps to her home, she caught sight of her little one on the porch, her baby boy, fussing in the packing box which served as cradle.

After the seeming eternity it took to get there, Lamb took the babe to her embrace and carried him inside for his breast feeding, oblivious to the interior work of Mrs. Ferree preparing the evening's meal of cooked beans to go along with the bread she had purchased downtown.

Then after Lamb's tendings of the child and the meal itself, Lamb rearranged the apron from her ankle length working clothes into a halter and placed the laughing child on her back. They would go for a romp out into the country in the waning minutes of light.

Soon the young mother, carrying her child, said good-bye to the Ferrees telling them she would return the next day after a night in the country. Lamb rarely left the home with this child for she had tried to keep his birth as secret as she could fearing the loss of her job if the plant owner, Mr. Rock, might learn he was employing an unwed mother of loose morals. But this one time she had to do so. She had to get away if only for this first time since the child's birth.

Oklahoma was not a place where one might easily have a secret life. There was no slipping in and out of town. The roads were barely a wagon- width wide in most places so any travel brought you close to the porches and front windows of every resi-dence along the street. If you were not announced by conversation and greeting, dogs would bark to give alarm and after their heraldry would follow the symphony of other animals in revelry, but the pigs squealing close to the houses were usually the most annoying.

Would the word spread that the girl living with the Ferrees appears to have a baby and be unwed? The baby's enclosure within Lamb's wide work apron would avoid that.

Soon the mother and child left the outskirts of the noisy work-ers' camp behind. The air was warm and inviting. How the camp had even grown in size this spring! Hundreds more were pouring in to Greenfield and many of these took up lives in the flimsy dwell-ings she was passing by.

The outskirts of Oklahoma was as a roughly vegetated field with bushy planty outgrowths sending brown stalks of wild grasses from their centers. Into this field some of the newer housing was nestled. Space was being made for displaced folk from Oklahoma's National Road frontage itself. Another Gas Boom industry, the East-side Glass Works, had recently begun the task of clearing away the workers' camp's own choicest spot, the northeast corner of the

National Road and Morristown Pike, for its new factory. Its residents had been pushed to these outskirts.

Lamb and her child would now escape toward the Hoosier fields of sweet-smelling spring hay. A path in front and behind and there upon its way a woman surrounded by the spring green of melding vegetation with a child within her hugging arms. There is no overgrowth here on this country slash with fields of planted crops coming up for viewing. Where the man holding this beautiful young mother's hand? Why does there seem so little hesitation to her step?

Close by a road she and her child passed a farmer's white-painted home. She heard the lady of the house say, "It's one of the mill girls" and she saw the man jump up from his wicker chair and shout to her, "Miss," he said, "you must see to getting home. The hour will soon be dark, and there have been reports that the Wild Bull has been seen in the neighborhood."

And yet on they walked, oblivious to the obvious danger, mother and child.

She walked with lighter steps down to the Panhandle Railroad, actually the nickname for the Indiana Central line, paralleling a route east and west and elevated slightly above the fields on each side. Lamb was on a journey seeking relief. She would avoid the further notice, like that of the nibby farm couple she had earlier passed, that came from traveling on the inhabited roads. The railroad tracks, a grade of crushed gravel, rock and cinders, had been forged from cut heavy stands of poplar, maples and oaks many years before. The growths of the young tree stands provided a shelter and comforting portal from the warm heaviness of this spring day. The branches were higher overhead where no passing train could trim them. They invaded the space above-appearing as friendly as arms extended in waving a greeting. The colors were so pleasant too, The bright leafy greens of the sun of the noon were softening into more earthy shades as the day was nearing its inevitable end. The path toward the East was as a tunnel within this growth of the newer, younger, more slender- trunked trees.

Up ahead on the tracks was a man who had not seen a good meal in days, perhaps weeks. Looking at him you would see a fellow of over 6 feet, strangely powerful appearing even if thin from his tramping. There was on his face the rangy, unkempt beard of one who takes no care to shave. His mustaches drooped to chin, untrimmed. Nor had he had a haircut within time recorded. Some would call the fellow a hobo.

He walked the tracks of the railways as did many others who were unemployed or shiftless. Usually, however, hobos walked in groups, most commonly three at a time. This fellow was alone - a mark that he did not brook company. His face mirrored the guess that he might be of sullen and lonely disposition. It was scarred as if he might have had reason not to want to be around others who would cast scorn at his horribly scarred face as well as his generally disreputable looking appearance.

His only baggage was the pole slung over his shoulder. A rag on its end contained a spare shirt, comb, beef cleaver for protection and personal items.

What was this? he wondered, as he saw Lamb carrying her child up ahead.

Lamb had not seen him as he slunk off into the track brush. He would let Lamb pass by the section of track where he was hiding. That way he could get a better look at this young woman who looked so beautiful to his sorely vexed eyes.

When Lamb passed him by on the Panhandle railroad tracks, he saw a beauty he had perhaps never, ever, seen before. Here before his very eyes and within his reach was the most beautiful girl in all the world.

And then Lamb was gone beyond his view.

The scarred fellow might rest in the brush, or he might drift on to the next town to beg a meal at a home there. He could do neither because the recollection of this defenseless young woman so close to him and so within his grasp remained in his mind and burned there with a feeling, a lust, that he had so rarely been able to control.

He wanted no trouble either. Most hobos knew better than to cause trouble. If one does, the mayor's courts of most of the towns along the railroad confine them to jail as quick as a wink. The scarred man knew that from firsthand knowledge. He had tested out bunks in most of the town jails along the Indiana Central and other lines.

Rather than go on, he would trail this beautiful young girl and see where she might go. It was so strange anyway! Here was such a beautiful creature and she was defenseless if he might want her. Yes, he wanted her. He would follow her and if she were asleep he might cover her eyes so that she could not identify him and have his own way. Yes, he decided to follow Lamb Hackleman to see where she might spend the night. If she was homeless as he was, and surely she was, she would have no protection from a quick advance. Since she had this baby with her, she was probably used to violation anyway!

Then, quietly, the scarred man began to trail his prey.

Up ahead Lamb reached the Range Line Road. Here the grassy cover was more profuse except where the winter's bite and the wind had occasionally hacked at the soil to uncover dirt, fallen leaves and bark, especially of the slippery hickory, and twigs and branches. Then Lamb walked south until she saw the familiar trussed timber span of bridge over Nameless Creek and crossed it before arriving at the farm of her girlhood along Dilly Creek, not that far, perhaps a mile, beyond. There, far back off the slash, was the home of her Hoosier Deutsch parents, a home she could never enter again.

Now out into a pasture the mother carrying her child flew, a field along the course of this tributary crick to Blue River, a magical place where the evening danced in wild play illuminated by a sky full of fireflies. Here was enchantment and another world.

The barely four-month-old child practiced a solemn walk, chubby hands holding on to his mother's, with mother in laughs of encouragement and embraces of pride. Soon enough the baby, understanding more, would be grown and informed by some stray word, some cruel laugh, some biting joke, to know his mother's heart had been filled with the love of a father he would never know.

Lamb had lost her heart. It had led her astray. Her secret was beyond explanation and a condemnation that followed her as a dark shadow every moment of her life except in such moments of escape as she now experienced. And what would the child think once he knew that his unwed mother conceived him in illegitimacy? The world of that shame would be back at Oklahoma, not here in the field of grass. Here for this brief moment Lamb could escape the ultimate fear and frustration of her life.

Now surrounded by the sweet smelling pasture, only recently cut for its hay, with its under grasses pushing up cushion for her escape, Lamb could forget about the coming time when her child would no longer look at her with love but with hate for the stigma of illegitimacy with which she had caused him to be cast. Here was a cow resting on the land with head raised to see who was coming. There a heifer, among others, standing on all fours with head grazing slowly across a stretch of grass. A spring calf stood beside its mother against a fenceline, the calf's nose a black button seen against its mother's reddish brown flank.

All of the world was soon taken into the grandeur and beauty of the darkness. Even the air. How could it be that the sky could blacken and fall with such power against the sun on the horizon dousing its fiery yellow into an ember of sinking orange? And there was no heavenly light.

Now, in the brilliance of the sky full of fireflies, Lamb shared the smiles which her child, Pleasant, so easily bestowed.

Until the coming time when her life would explode, Lamb Hackleman would devote her every available moment to this child of her love, knowing that time was her enemy, that after the march of days she must lose this child to his certain rejection of her for who she was, an unwed mother, and what she had made him, a bastard.

Then came the time when the child and her mother could no longer grope to the romp. The child fell asleep in his mother's arms. And then too Lamb welcomed the night from closing eyes. The night was not only an outside force but a force which had struck within her soul. She might forego much and would for the care of her child, but would not there be a single ray of hope for her and the man who had held her and caught her heart in a net beyond freeing? No. Yet would she fall asleep and sink further into the symphony of the blackness and night that was all there was within her hearing.

But the fireflies revealed other activity as well. As Lamb lay quietly with Pleasant aside, the scarred man came out from the crick growth where he had kept his ward and watch, awaiting the right moment to come on to Lamb to have his way with her and then escape.

The man made scarcely a noise as he continued his approach.

Only one mistake had he made. He had invaded the crick country of the Wild Bull of Blue River. He was in another's lair, one who he could never have expected.

Wild Bull had just been on the approach to Lamb himself. He had been down crick and had not yet completed his rounds of the places where his beloved Lamb might be waiting. With surprise and joy, Wild Bull had seen Lamb this very night after all the other nights of late when his rounds had been fruitless.

But as the Wild Bull began to draw close to Lamb, imagine his consternation to find his approach was shared by another character, this one looking exceedingly seedy and dangerous. Wild Bull had seen this kind of guy before on his wanderings. He had a run in with hobos before. Once some had looked at him as steak while he was wandering down the tracks himself. Wild Bull had come away with a distinct dislike for hobos out of that engagement.

Then Wild Bull noticed that Lamb might be this fellow's prey. Wild Bull would never have allowed a wolf or panther or bear to come onto Lamb and he suddenly increased this list of "no access" to hobos.

Unfortunately the scarred man's desire for Lamb did not allow him to be deterred easily. As the man closed in, even seeing the Wild Bull ominously near, he kept on his offense.

By the time he and Wild Bull were near to each other, there had been no turning back. The man would beat him away to get to Lamb, but Wild Bull was not to be brushed away by anyone who might mean Lamb harm. The hobo decided to up the stakes. He pulled his meat cleaver from his little pack and waved it in the air as if to worn the Wild Bull that he should not charge. The weapon was formidable and certainly was designed for beef such as the Wild Bull. The meat cleaver's blade was a foot long and half again as wide. It still bore a shred of the twine braided within the hole in its upper corner where the former owner had hung it in his shed where he did his butchering. The scarred man had found it there and had broken the twine it was strung on with his good teeth. The handle was only long enough for a hand to grasp. The weapon had seen its better days. Most of it was rusty from lack of care. But its blade could hack much harm. As the man wielded his cleaver, so did the Wild Bull wave his horns into the air to warn off the hobo.

Neither was frightened from the conflict. Wild Bull lowered his horns to charge. There came a scramble and the meat cleaver was lost on the ground. Its one swing in the air had missed the mark and the swing had been too exaggerated for the man to regain control. The Wild Bull got the better of the business. Later, the injured man, arising from the ground, held his gored stomach with his hands, unable to hold back the pouring blood, and took to the run to reach the other side of Dilly Crick. Wild Bull followed and saw the scarred man break his fall into the crick with his head and remain submerged under the heavy and deep crick waters. The man's face beneath the waters showed the terror of starring eyes unfocusable. The opened mouth was welcoming the entry of new and untried food, waters which were elementally unprejudiced. Whatever had been the countenance of a man was now contorted into the face of a corpse. After a short time, the Wild Bull saw the man's lifeless body listlessly begin its float downstream. How odd the thin wave of bloody froth that followed after him!

Only then, when there seemed no possibility of further harm to Lamb, did Wild Bull go back to where Lamb was asleep, unaware that a danger had come close.

And so now, silently appearing, another form now approached the sleeping mother and son, a Wild Bull, nosing close and scanning the scene for any other trouble which might lurk or threaten.

This creature was not one to harm despite his recent engagement. The Wild Bull of Blue River took to his position resting close beside to keep the mother and her poor child in sight, and to safeguard them through the dark hours of the night, providing protection from every black shadow or any person or beast who might mean them harm.

When Lamb awoke it was Sunday morning and here she was...in the lair of the Wild Bull of Blue River and he by her side along with her child.

"Oh Wild Bull," Lamb said upon opening her eyes and finding the Wild Bull close. Then leaving her baby to the warming sod and a hasty straw cradle of the meadow pasture, she arose to throw her arms around this creature. "I knew you would be here! I knew it!"

She and the Wild Bull went down to the crick, not far away, where they had wandered so often in their youths. "I had to come show you my child and talk." The Wild Bull looked back at the baby and nodded his head with approval.

"Oh, Wild Bull," she said, "You are all that I have of a past. I have no one and nothing else for family but you."

Truth to tell, Lamb had been busting out with pride about this child of hers for weeks, awaiting the right warm weekend when she might return to the cricklands to tell the Wild Bull about her child. She would have this one weekend only and then she would not return again, perhaps forever, but this one Sunday would be hers to spend in a romp with the Wild Bull and her child in the secret places of the Blue River where she had known youth and love.

"Where did this child come from?" Wild Bull seemed to want to know.

"Well, you see, I work at a paper mill now," Lamb explained. "it is good work, but hard, and my wages bear my son's and my keep so I cannot lose this job!"

Wild Bull understood fully.

"It was in February, Wild Bull," she went on to explain. "I knew the child was due from how tender my breasts had become. I felt as flush as the burning fires of my pulp digester at the mill. I really did. And then I felt contractions."

"At the mill? While you were working?" the Wild Bull wanted to know.

"Yes," Lamb admitted, "but if they had known I was even pregnant they would have fired me on the spot! I still must keep this child from their notice."

Wild Bull felt sympathy for her dilemma.

"Anyway," she said, "I rushed back to my home in Oklahoma and gave birth to this child you see in front of you within the hour of my return. This little boy is named Pleasant. At birth he was so pink! I was in dreadful pain, but when I heard him sneeze out of a little wrinkly nose, I had to laugh anyway, despite the pain. Mrs. Ferree helped me. She is the lady of the house where I live and a very nice person," Lamb went on to add.

Wild Bull was surely pleased to know that.

She would not burden Wild Bull with the rest of the story...how she had brought the child to her breast for the first time and felt the child and her join together in the exciting enterprise of his first meal. Nor would she tell the Wild Bull how hard it was the next morning to go back to the mill before dawn and leave the child to the care of the Ferrees. How much more she would have preferred to stay at the home with this new child of hers. But she would have to keep the secret of the child's birth to herself and the Ferrees...except now she had been able to give the news to the Wild Bull.

She and Wild Bull would take a morning walk and then after feeding Pleasant she would go to the places along the crick which were so strongly in her memory, places where she had been with her young man.

She sat down quietly on a rock beside the restless crick waters.

"Wild Bull," she said softly to her companion beside her, "one of these days I shall lose this child as I have lost the man. One of these days, the child will know me only as an unwed mother who has cast upon him the mantle of bastardy. Then he will blame me and leave me and I will be alone again."

The minutes of solitude were passing quickly and soon she would have to return to her child left in its play close to the bed of hay within view. The late morning shadows were lengthening every object.

Lamb looked at Wild Bull desperately. "Why does there have to be condemnation in this world! Why no redemption from its anger? Why cannot the world be kind and love prevail every minute?"

Her life seemed such a heavy weight!

"When I was a child, I thought love was everywhere," she told the Wild Bull. "I could see it in the eyes of my mother and father with their every look. I could see it too in the eyes of my beloved. Now I see it no where at all. Was I just a child to believe there was such a thing as love in this world?"

Only in the early afternoon did she agree with Time that she must leave the lair of the Wild Bull to return to Oklahoma. The walk home with Pleasant was under the warm sun and blue sky. She must arise the next morning before dawn to go to the mill. She felt no need to apologize to anyone for taking this digression from her days at the mill. She had wished the Wild Bull to know of the child. She had had to tell someone. She could not show the child to its father or her parents, mother or father. She would instead proudly show the child to the Wild Bull of Blue River for there was no one else.

And she would continue to wonder where, if anywhere, was love.

5

A Dead Man In Blue River

It was later on in the next year of 1894, on a beautiful Sunday morning in June to be more exact, that a dead man's body was found floating in Blue River. The news spread in the Hoosier Deutsch countryside, throughout Hancock County, and the Blue River Valley. The information frightened everyone.

A man of God made the gruesome discovery of the Wild Bull's latest trick. The Wild Bull had finally done it! Killed a man! The victim's hideously decomposing body had been found moving uneasily in the Blue River. Fear spread. The Bull might be on a rampage.

It was a Sunday morning and the discovery should not have taken place as it did. The discoverer of the body was this very unlikely fellow, an itinerant preacher who was hurrying on his way from his last charge up to the white- boarded Gilboa Methodist in its heavily wooded setting in the sloping land of the Hoosier back country. The gawky and awkward looking old fellow, bearded down to a spade below his chin, was actually the preacher, Brother Aultman.

Here he was so enjoying the beauteous scene of land in accordant colors. Spring had given the earth over to the young hues of green signaling growth and rebirth, hope and renewal. Life was in its triumphant hours now that it was spring and the discordant days of winter where windy howls might mix with snowy gusting were over. The land seemed so at peace. Not even the spoked wheels of the pastor's buggy, creaking and whirring as they did, could disturb the peaceful sound of soft river whispering. God was in the heavens over this place. All was well even though Brother Aultman was thinking how hard it was to be a good man of God when you might be late for services.

The Godly man had been reining in his horse to stay on the running boards of the wooden bridge over Blue River when, just before he entered the bridge's cover, he happened to look down at the sluggish brown river to notice a buoyant lump in the water. He couldn't see much - what looked like shoulders and a head shape - but it was enough for him to imagine that it was a person.

Pulling his buggy to the roadside, the old man had fought his way through the tangles of thistles and young scrub tree brush to arrive at the banks of the river. The preacher's lanky legs made him look rather foolish in fiddling around in the river, especially so since his bright and stiff black suit legs were pulled up hurriedly. That a man in such a formal outfit, wearing white shirt and white bow tie under heavily starched collar, would go for a wade made the scene appear ludicrous. But out in the water the fellow went and then, after he had got himself good and wet, thought the better of it and got back on shore. Anyway, while out there, he had been close enough to know what he had seen. There, near a sand island, where the river narrowed to avoid entering the main channel just upstream from the bridge, the preacher confirmed the grisly discovery. Not more than two feet away he had seen the scarred face of a dead man swollen to bursting. But he had best get back to the bank. No point in angering the mudpuppies slithering through the waters and capable of rendering nasty bites. Once back on the shore, man of God or not, he must fish the body out hurriedly, remembering that he was due at the Gilboa Church any time. He snapped off a corkscrew willow limb and to avoid falling into the muddiness of the river headfirst while he was making his pull he began fishing at the body with the limb until its branches reached the dead man's far side so that his bloated body could be raked closer. In this way, the minister was able to draw the dead fellow to the shore. The corpse was heavy and waterlogged as the river water had entered his blood system bullying its way in, expanding the veins and arteries to explosion, killing the man's red blood cells so as to turn his complexion into the whiteness of snow.

Then, Brother Aultman was able to drag the rotten form of the man from the water to the shore by pulling at the corpse's arm, until its head, with eyes and mouth open, was pulled up to grass, scratched by the resisting bank twigs all the way up the muddy slope.

Once on shore, the preacher did what examining he could.

It was not possible to tell how the long the man had been dead. Ordinarily, when drownings proceed, the body sinks at first and does not rise bloating for some time, maybe months, and in this case further complication came from the bruising movement of the churning river buffeting the body about from shore rock to catch of fallen trees in the river to new engagement with something distorting.

Turning over the body, gashes into its front became evident. Something had torn at the man's coat, ripping at it and tearing away flesh as by a knife or steely horn. Some of the flesh around the stomach appeared to be gauged out as if by being horned.

A movement caught his eye while he was there, hunched over near the dead form, trying both to support himself and avoid becoming sick. It was a movement upstream.

The Wild Bull it was! or so he would have sworn. By his account, its head was tossing and its breath pluming steamy and triumphantly in the hot summer air on the other bank. He remembered the Wild Bull staring at him coldly as if to say, "You're next, Buddy!" Even a man of God doesn't want to answer that call.

Quickly leaving the body on the bank of the river in a scadaddle, Brother Aultman hurried to his buggy, snapped his horse to break into trot, and was on his way to his next Sunday morning charge. Nothing was ever so welcome to him as the sight of the steeple of the Gilboa Church, or rather its slatted box, concaving into a point with its little wooden cross on top, appearing above the trees near its clearing. It didn't take him long to enter the church doors either and close them tight.

At the Gilboa Church, he opened his service with a quick prayer.

"The Devil himself may be in this neighborhood," he began, and only then related the reason for his tardiness in arriving at the church. Was he referring to the Wild Bull? Many later thought so and it is believed that this was the source of the widely held belief in the Deutsch countryside during these days that the Wild Bull was actually the Devil.

Anyway, the Wild Bull had finally been proven to be a killer who had horned some unlucky person - who it was no one knew - would they ever know? - who had invaded his lair.

The preacher's church service proceeded with the exception that a couple of the young men quietly left the church service upon hearing the news that a dead man's body had been found which would require investigation.

These young men were a kernel of the neighborhood posse who sometimes called their informal organization a "Horse Thief Detective Company" to bring it under the Indiana law permitting citizens to assume police duties.

In this era in Indiana there was no law enforcement in the back country. The peacekeepers - what law there was -were the young men of the neighborhoods deputized by the necessity of safeguarding horses and livestock from thieves and rustlers or other felons.

Two of these were the men who left the church service to contact others and soon there was a motley gathering of many of the neighborhood men. The gathering point was at their usual meeting place, the Sipe farm on the second slash south of the National Road. To look at them you would merely see young, stubbly-jawed Hoosier Deutsch farmers of the area, mostly in their late teens or twenties, riding their snorting horses into a pack to learn of the news and decide what to do.

If you lived in the neighborhood, you might have recognized in the center of the gathering Michael Sipe. Also if you knew Michael, you might recognize his chestnut horse as well. Red was his name. He was not a fancy horse but rather one of stock type and quarter bred. Carrying Michael at a walk was no burden for the horse because Michael was not heavy but of an athletic and slim build. Michael and Red in fact knew each other well from daily enterprises. Michael knew the rhythm of his Red's gait and Red always cocked his ears to the rear for the hearing of his rider's every command as they faced their duties together. Red too was an inquisitive horse and kept his eyes peeled to the road and any movement ahead or to the side so that though Red's head remained at a level with his back his alert eyes proved him anything but a mere plodder.

No posse would have been called without notifying Michael Sipe. He was the leader of the young men in the neighborhood and a Thor of a person, sharply staring through blue eyes and boasting long brown hair down to his shoulders that flowed behind as if from a breeze when he was mounted and bearing out on his flushed horse. His was the commanding appearance before whom the others deferred.

"Let's go see the murder scene," Michael Sipe told the mounted posse when the group appeared to have contained its complement. Fifteen or twenty were present. Some of them pulled out their shotguns or other weapons for loading or cocking. At the direction, the young men gave their mounts their heads to go to the nearby bridge over Blue River.

At the wooden bridge the posse located the corpse, dismounted and looked closely at the scarred man's wounds.

Then, one after another, the posse took hold of their saddle horns and swung up to their mounts. They had seen enough. Soon all feet were in stirrups except Michael's. The men brought their horses to an irregular circle around him to receive their instructions.

Michael pointed out the sectors each should cover and had them filter out into the country and along its back river up country paths in search of clues as to the mystery and to check in the neighborhood to see if a man was missing at an upstream home. It was passed around that, sure enough, this fellow must have been the victim of a goring by the Wild Bull of Blue River. One after another they left, this one riding tight, that one fanning his horse with his hat, another hanging on with his knees. One of the young men stuck his chin in the air and tore out like he was coming out of a bucking chute waving a colt .44 six shooter in the air and yelling back to the others it was he who would bring back the points of the Wild Bull to answer for the crime. Others laughed, scoffing at his bravado.

The group would shoot twice in the air if any found danger or wished the aid of the others. Else they would just go home and leave Michael with the task of returning with his wagon to take the body into Greenfield to the coroner.

Now the work would be the lonely one of the individuals of the posse asking at the farms if a man of the house was missing or seeking other clues.

Even while the posse was investigating, the talk abounded. The talk was that the Wild Bull might now be on a bloodlust.

Many started to remember other bodies found near the river or its tributary cricks, or other blobs in the water that had been seen but had not been investigated for what they might have been - victims of a bloody murderer now universally held to be the Wild Bull.

How about Willie Shultz who was missing from his young wife, the Trees girl? Or Wolf Kuhn who had taken to babbling in drunkenness, no longer even speaking sense? Was the cause an encounter with the Devil? The Wild Bull?

All this was in the context of no one seeing the Wild Bull commit any crime. But while due process may rule the course of human justice, animals do not, apparently, deserve its presumptions. Circumstantial evidence kept accumulating proving the Wild Bull a murderer whose guilt was established beyond a reasonable doubt.

And even as the neighborhood posse was out in the search for clues as to the death and the identity of the man, the Wild Bull held the Blue River roads and traces in terror, a fact over which no human being had control.

6

Michael Sipe's Search

Michael Sipe stayed behind after the other young men of the horse thief detective company had ridden off on their steeds in various directions fanning out over the Blue River Valley neighborhood. They were on a mission. Michael, their leader, had assigned each of them an area in which to make enquiry. Perhaps one of the young Deutschmen in the posse might learn who it was who had been found dead in Blue River, bobbing in a grotesque scene, until pulled out of the water by the preacher, Brother Aultman.

But many of the young men had another mission and that was to stay alive in the byways of the Blue River woods where the Wild Bull roamed, or kill the Wild Bull if they came across it while doing their posse work.

There was probably not a single one of them who had not heard the thrashings of the Wild Bull in the woods and yet not one, though he be the finest hunter in Indiana, could zero in for the kill. The Wild Bull knew the woods better than any of them. None could hunt it down, not even with the best tracking gear, nor could they ever stalk the Wild Bull's movements as it turned and blew like the wind from place to place over a terrain the Wild Bull obviously knew so well. It was like trying to follow a tornado. You can't. It hits and destroys and then lifts to jump over a farm before devastating a fence row on the next place over or worse, a farmhouse, before lifting to conserve its force in order to mow down a woods. The rough land and marshes and wet spots along Blue River gave the bull sanctuary and made tracking it impossible.

Still, as the stout young Deutschmen of the posse began their mission, Michael Sipe stayed behind.

Michael just stood there at the site of the recovery of the bloated body. He was now strangely quiet in the early afternoon brightness eschewing the shade of the nearby wooden covered bridge. The spring air was busy with life and yet for the longest time this handsome fellow, the accepted leader of the neighborhood's peacekeepers, this bright-eyed young farmer responsible for all the 160 acres of the Sipe farm, one of the area's most productive and well kept, did not speak or even move.

Michael merely stood by the river which might have appeared a mirror if all of the spring colors had not interfered. He did not fit into the picture of the greens of the trees, shrubs and shore grasses, from the yellowish ones to the dark greenish blue, each imposing upon the waters its hues. The river could not run swiftly enough to escape their patchwork reflective blanketing. Nothing from below, creatures of the muddy bottom, not even the more actively swimming fish and crustacean, could so disturb the surface as to alter the patterning created by the unintended reflections of the green bank growths. Only the blue uncluttered sky could influence the patching with occasional blues rendered shiny and bright by the glancing of the sun's hot rays across the sky. And yet Michael stood by the river's banks, his mind seeking a calm that could not be found.

Then Michael looked down at the unrecognizable corpse on the bank of the river and shook his head. "How I wish that I were you," he finally said in a whisper.

What strange words coming from this young man!

Finally, Michael too mounted his horse, jammed his shotgun into its leather casing aside the saddle and snapped the reins. He would leave the scene now as had the others and ride toward the area he had assigned himself to investigate.

After crossing the bridge he reined his horse to take a trail down to the river along its northern bank ironically ranged with forget-me- nots, partly in and partly out of the water. He was on a journey into madness. He would return through the crickland of the Dilly Crick where he had known and loved Lamb Hackleman, the young neighbor girl, with an impossible love the depth of which he could not fathom.

The ride would take him through the remaining wilds of the land. Except for these Blue River woods, most of Indiana was now, in the 1890s, under cultivation, much drained by the surface ditching that came to enter the streams. Occasionally there would be a field of corn, or less often, wheat and oats, that extended all the way to the river or its cricks. But the depressions and the hollows carved out by the flowing streams kept their wild appearance even in this day and age.

In much of its extent the depressions through which the river and cricks wound had been given over to livestock. Such farms might have hayfields of clover and timothy visible through the covering woods.

The thoughts of Michael were these.

And now she was gone! Why had Lamb Hackleman left him? Her mother had told him she had returned to live with her cousins at the Deutsch settlement at Hellam, Pennsylvania. No communication there, however, please! How could he have known the loss of her presence would leave him as he now was, hopelessly broken in heart, sick to his very soul.

His mind was not on his business. But if he had taken note as would have any of the other posse members, he might have begun to hear the familiar thrashings about that struck terror in the hearts of so many. For to his side, his ride was being noticed by the little beady eyes of Terror itself on hooves.

Michael would follow the Blue River to its junction with Dilly Crick and ask around that tributaries' residents for information about anyone missing. It was an area he was familiar with because the Sipe farm was next off the crick, separated from it only by the equally large Hackleman farm.

The ride should have been pleasant and enjoyable and in a way it was. The Blue River's trails wound through turns and bends, places of constant surprise and natural beauty. There in a break of sunlit space might be Dwarf Iris or Bee Balm in profusion. If ever there is a time of year when Hancock County lavishes itself in beauty it is the spring. It is a time of blooming and renewal.

And the life river of it was all the beautiful Blue River. Blue River was not cultivated all the way to its banks. Its curves and bends followed the gentle roll of the land itself so that often the mud of the river and the mud of its banks could not even be differentiated. This was not a river through a gorge or one which cut canyons through rock. It sought no separate identity apart from the farm land it drained or its simple and humble Hoosier Deutschfolk, living quiet lives of industry and peace in a nearly level land or gently undulating till plain, crisscrossed by morainic ridges and shallow drainage ways derived from Ice Age meltings. It was a supportive river, a helper, one fit to relax on, fish for log perch, sunfish, blackstripes, brook shiners, golden redhorses, suckers, or mullets, especially in the warming spring days of April.

It gave the land its identity. One could say he lived in the Blue River country. The river was as a playground of a place to wander, but sometimes the bushes and thistles along its banks made traveling difficult. Its sand bars were deceiving too. A step on what would appear firm ground would cause you to sink a foot down into mud.

But the scene was a familiar one to Michael. He could not become moved in its mysteries because it bore his memories of his life, now foundering more and more into the past, with Lamb Hackleman. He almost could sense her presence here and yet she was not there.

Then, as Michael entered the crick trail which bordered the Hackleman farm, the impossible happened. There up ahead of him stood the Wild Bull of Blue River as if awaiting him.

How could this be? Here the killer himself!

Here, up ahead, was a catch which had eluded every catcher, a hunted one come out into the open, the Wild Bull of Blue River.

We remember that the hunters with the shiniest new shotguns or smooth bored rifles had tried to track it down to shoot it even before its reputation as the killer of the drowned man had raced around the land. Each wanted the trophy of those Hereford horns to show his neighbors and friends. In fact, if any succeeded, that one would truly have become a local hero, much as becomes the high school basketball player who shoots the winning basket for the Sectional championship and is proudly borne on the shoulders of his high school teammates around the gymnasium, and whose efforts become the stuff of heroic legend. Others might have deer horns, or antelope, or caribou, with points innumerable and massive, mounted on plaques in their dens. Some fishermen might have the gaping mouth of a 20 pound pike tacked on a shed, or the stretch of a 5 foot muskie, or photo of an 8 pound bass or walleye, on their wall. But who might boast of such a prize as the steel-like points of a Wild Bull which had terrorized a whole stretch of Indiana valley country?

Michael saw him as the beast came toward him, but he drew no weapon. He watched with his saddened eyes as the beast approached closer and closer.

Then Michael dismounted as the animal came to him. The two stood together drinking in each's presence with the other in a scene of familiarity and trust. Then, Michael bent to pick some meadow grass and took it to the beast who looked up at this friendly man and shook his head as if to invite a frisk before coming close to accept the gift. Then, together the two walked the scene of their romps only this time without Lamb Hackleman.

The Wild Bull was the pet of Michael's beloved.

The Wild Bull missed her as much as he did.

What had happened to Lamb? Michael asked the bull, knowing no beast or person, for that matter, could provide him the answer. What had happened to his life? He guided his horse behind him with the reins loose in his hand as he walked toward the waters of Dilly Crick, the Wild Bull by his side. Then he wrapped his reins around a yellow blooming spicebush. He would go look into the crick there thinking to himself as he went how nothing could ever be forever. Life escapes as does water rushing downstream. He should never have expected that he might have Lamb Hackleman to love eternally. It was he who was at fault. Everything went wrong for him and the only way his life might have gone right would have been if he could have had Lamb as his wife. Maybe it was his expectation that had driven him down. How could he have expected that

Lamb might love him. Why was he always wanting more than he could have?

If he had known that she must leave him, he might have played their relationship differently. He would not have invested so in his heart now crushed and broken.

He went over to sit on the chair of the lower branch of one of the twin sycamores where he had been with Lamb Hackleman so often. Not even the brightness of the Jack-in-the-pulpits and clusters of yellow Lady's-slippers could brighten his mood. How he would have given his very life to have her there with him again, to win just a few more moments with her from jealous time itself.

The Wild Bull of Blue River lay by his side. There in the wilds of the Blue River back country, the Thor of the neighborhood dropped his face into his hands and wept. The Wild Bull could do no more than come to him and closely nudge him while Michael lifted his head to look into the beast's eyes, then rubbed under his massive head. "Did she need her freedom as much as you do?" he said. "Should I not have wished to be everything to her?"

He would stay only moments more in this enchanted place where he had loved the girl, where he could remember how it felt to fall in love, and be with the one he loved, before he would now have to remount his horse and ride up the ridge of Dilly Crick to the Hackleman home to complete his mission for the posse. Reaching the heights of any slope from the crick always required Red, Michael's horse, to heave his shoulders and draw deep breaths with relief and a couple of good pants in full measure. Now both rider and mount drew deep breaths of air as they gained the ridge within sight of the home of the Hacklemans and the former home of Lamb. Michael's breath was anguished for he could not return to the lair of the Wild Bull to find there the girl who could alone calm his world with her gentle smile.

7

Birth Of The Wild Bull

Six years before the discovery of the bloated body floating in Dilly Crick, there had been a winter still talked about.

It seems that every year, in January, or perhaps February, even today, there strikes a blow of killing cold in the Hoosier Deutschlands. Such a time occurred in the January of 1888 when the freezing breath of the north wind was wheezed out over the land. It was a time of shivering and a chill to the bones of person and beast.

There must have been over three inches of snow on the ground, enough to cover the earth's every blemish. Such a snow turns nature into a strange sculptress. Shapes of it cause you to dread what it represents. The drifts and blowings seem so beautiful by day but strange and fearfully unrecognizable, portending the dangers of the unknown, at night. Even during the day the branches of bushes bend with the snowy load and break to the earth in surrender. When there is cold also, below zero weather such as accompanied the snow at this January, the snow is a white bleeding as it clings not only to the tops of injured limbs but somehow adheres also to their sides in defiance of gravity.

The night cold becomes a danger and a stalker for prey. It hangs like an unseen ghost prepared to use the snow as a pillow to smother any it can hold, carrying its freezing power ominously over the white meadow pasture. Any who might walk through it had best fear throttling. Steps crinkle and snap as if the snow were ice, except after each step, the snow kicks away in front and behind in small powdery explosions.

Lamb Hackleman had been 12 then, during this period of seasonal weather, hardly old enough to stay outside long in such weather at all.

And yet she did go out with her father, a farmer with livestock, to the barn on such days when the cattle came up from the crick pastures for their evening feeding of hay and to stay in the shelter of the barn for the night.

The barn itself - three levels under gambreled roof -was an imposing structure behind the Hackleman home and on the ridge above Dilly Crick. It was perfectly designed for its many uses. It sheltered the cattle at its lowest level. The Hackleman's cattle herd, 15 strong, could reach it by the easily navigated path up the 20 foot grade from the crick. The crick watered the herd. Then also, the barn served as a threshing floor, grainery and machine shed on the cavernous main level. At the front of this main floor were the horse stalls for the work animals of the farm. Behind the barn, to its south, was the primary hayfield. Hay could be readily transported from the hayfield to the barn's forschuss, or projection out over the ground floor. Other grain could be easily stored in the barn as well. The corn fields, where Lemuel Hackleman still husked his corn by hand from the standing stalks, were on the other side of the crick not far away -as were the wheat fields - and were reached by the ford over Dilly Crick at the foot of its ridge. The outside of the barn was boarded except for the north side where field stone covered the exterior in the traditional "stone to the weather" Deutsch manner.

The farm horses, needed for pulling Lemuel's new metal plow, his metal-tooth harrow and cultivator with its small shovels, stayed most often in the extensive barnlot while the cattle would frequently graze the long crick meadow, running the length of the farm, north to south, and cutting it into two, down beneath the barn. The cattle spent their days by the crick even on these winter days taking wind cover from its crick sycamores and willows, or grazing with "back to wind."

The barn was not only a busy place in the winter with cattle seeking its nightly asylum, it was also a busy place for Lemuel Hackleman, Lamb's father, throughout the year. Anna would often complain that Lemuel was out in the barn more than he was in the house.

There was purpose in his labors and both knew it. All the summer long before, and the fall, too, Lemuel had planned for such a chill as this one in January. Planning ahead was the way of the industrious and careful Deutsch farmers of the Blue River Valley. Lemuel's hay mow was filled. Many of the preceding warm days, Lemuel had spent out in the fields of timothy and the sweet smelling clover cutting and gathering the hay with a horse drawn dump rake owned in partnership with his neighbors, the Sipes, pitching it into a wagon by hand and loading it into the loft from his horse-drawn farm wagon.

On this bitterly cold night loomed the haunting question-What could have happened to the brood cow Trinka? She did not report to the barn for the evening's hay with the rest of the herd.

Unfortunately Lemuel did not even notice her absence.

Lamb had not missed her either, not until after both father and daughter had returned to the house after performing their nightly feeding, and in fact not until Lamb had been tucked into her bed by her mother, Anna.

But then it had come to her. One of the brood cattle had not been with the herd this night! It was Trinka she had not seen! The thought had come to her suddenly and left her restless.

By the time she had decided she would go out to the barn to confirm her fear, her parents had retired for the night to their upstairs bedroom. She did not dare to awaken them.

Slipping on her coat, Lamb went out into the black night with only the kerosene lamp that her father kept by the back door.

In the barn, she confirmed the absence of Trinka from the others. But where could she be? Lamb decided she would go see if Trinka were in the meadow, discounting the danger of the weather without sufficient thought.

Lamb knew the Dilly Crick meadow as she knew the back of her hand.

With only the company of the light of her father's kerosene lantern, Lamb went down the path from the barn ridge to the crick meadow on a search calling for Trinka in her voice with which all the cattle were familiar.

Up above were the eternal stars which shine as witnesses to all events, those of desperation as well as those of comfort, always reminding that there is light even in darkness.

Lamb crossed the rock-filled ford to search the lower meadow. Just on the other side of the iced over crick, at the foot of an embankment, she saw a cow. The path of its fall was visible. It must have attempted to negotiate the cliff over the crick underlain with sand that had given way.

There on her side in brokenness lay the wounded cow, her white face a blend to the snow itself with only her ears arched in keeping a silent last alert. She could not arise to give any more greeting. Her back had been broken and her legs could not lift her to arise. Daggers of icy wind were stabbing her in her helpless state. Lamb immediately recognized the scene as one of hopelessness.

And then another image occurred. A small brown package. Was it a calf? What if Trinka was calving! It should not have been. The brood cows were bred to calve in the spring. But what if something had gone wrong and the brood cow had calved out in this weather? Often with the Herefords it is hard to tell if they are ready to calve.

Was this the reason that Trinka had not gone up to the barn with the other cattle? Sometimes cows did this, staying out in the pasture to give birth. But if so, her calf could never survive such cold. Even so, it was not the instinct of cattle to bring their calves to barns, but rather to hide them where only the mother might find them.

And yes at her back was a calf born into the desperation of the night. Lamb rushed to it over the iced-over crick, not thinking how dangerous might be her venture if the ice had given way to her weight. Yes, the calf was still warm. She picked it up and took it into its mother's view. No, the brood cow could not lick to clean it up. And the mother's look said to her calf, "How could I have known I would have to leave you this way? How could I have known that I might misstep. Was it a muskrat tunnel into the bank that I stepped in trying to bear you in a special place where you and I might share your first moments alone? How can I leave you, and yet I must, even knowing you need me so!" And then the eyes lost the brightness of their look at the little calf the cow had birthed in such dire circumstances.

Lamb had little time to consider what to do after her discovery of the calf, born so shortly before and after the fall, with every ounce of energy the broken brood cow had managed to muster.

Lamb knew she had work she must do there on the sandy bank within the curve of the disturbed cut of earth and beside the icy waters. No matter that her knuckles were white from the cold and she was losing feeling in her fingers. She would do the work that the farm women of livestockers know how to do and have done over the generations. She would clean the little calf and bite off its umbilical cord.

The one essential task was to feed the calf its first milk from the mother. Despite the bitter cold and the forbidding circumstances, the colostrum of the brood calf containing its special potion of nutrients and doses of protective natural medicines must be given the calf. The alternative is death. Killer infections have no heart. And the dying brood cow gave of its last for the little calf while the little girl said to her, "Don't worry, Trinka, I will keep your child warm. He will live within my protection and I will love him as I love my very own life."

Then as Lamb picked up the frightened calf from the shelter of her mother's last warmth and first and last feeding, she held the calf within the shelter of her own coat for a windbreaking. As they left, the brood cow took a final look at the two, the little calf of her own being and the little girl, and yielded herself to the way of death and saw no more. Soon the warmth of her body fled into the night air. Her last hearing would be of her calf bawling into the killing, below-zero winds for requiem.

It was difficult enough for Lamb to make her own way through the meadow in the raging cold, but she would now do something further that she must. She would also carry an unexpected burden, this calf, to safety. Yet do it she would. She would take care of this young calf born out of season and in such danger. She would dare fate itself and establish for all time that love does not die. She would become the parent of this calf herself, taking the place of this beast whose own life with the calf was a dream which could not be.

She would go to her father's barn. Here she would make her stand for life with this calf. She would find a corner of the barn protected and out of the wind chill. The hexes on each of the stone side ends of the barn would bear her good luck.

There in the barn, settled within a fortress of hay. Lamb held the little calf to herself, its long legs helplessly hanging from her young girl's grasp. Smiling at the little calf, holding it to herself, warming it with her own body, she swore to the night cold and life itself through its guardian stars above that this calf would grow within her care and love, and that she would see its life would be one of endless wonder. And then, she pledged herself to stay even though the wintry night would seek her out to kill her and her charge with its hug of cold!

Not until the morning light would she relinquish her calf and then she made her further vow. This little one would never be cut as the young male calves were to turn them into steers. This calf would never be fed out and taken to market, either. This calf would be her companion forever and ever and live as in fantasy, freely, as the Prince of the Land. This calf would not be as the others of her father's herd. She would hold up this calf to the light. Its life would be as charmed as she could make it, this little unexpected spirit whose birth suggested the strange ways of providence itself.

By the time morning gilded the sky, Lamb had taken him downstream to another place of natural shelter at another crick spot where no person tred, a secret world, a place where not even her father or mother would know. And so had been born and raised the Wild Bull of Blue River even as the little girl became a woman.

8
Lamb's Sin

Michael Sipe, the saddened, handsome young neighbor boy and leader of the horse thief detective company, dismounted, tied his horse, Red, at the hitch, and went to the back door of the Hackleman home on Dilly Crick.

The Hackleman's place was the last stop of his appointed area for investigation in the Hoosier back country. Still, he had gained no clue to the identity of the dead man found floating in Blue River on that June, 1894, Sunday. But the truth was that this investigation was not important to him anyway and the last thing on his mind.

Michael had not chosen this area in which to make enquiry accidentally. He had wanted to stop at the Hackleman home with all his heart. Miracles do happen. Perhaps Lamb Hackleman, his beloved, the strangely absent daughter of the Hackleman home, might be there. Or perhaps her parents might volunteer some news? Even the slightest word of her might restore him to life. How had he been able to get along these long, past few impossible months without her? His days were as a bad dream from which he could not awake. How could Lamb have left without even saying good-bye!

Michael knocked at the back door. The door opened into the kitchen. The Hackleman house could be thought of as two rectangular boxes conjoined under a gabled interconnecting roof. The front rectangular box was the smaller in width, about thirty feet. It was two story and it faced the road although separated from it by an extensive woods and farm pond in front. The second rectangular box was the back side of the home, one story, but wider, about forty feet, the extra width accommodating the huge kitchen that Anna had wanted when the new home replaced Lemuel's parents' widened log cabin.

When Michael Sipe's knock came on the back kitchen door, Anna Hackleman heard it from her daughter's, Lamb Hackleman's, bedroom, next to the huge kitchen. She went to the window to look out to see who was knocking.

Anna was a small woman, hardly 5 foot, with every appearance of wear, burden and anxiety. Anna always seemed to have a purse and draw to her lips these days, as if her lips were set tightly to hold all words of peace until another time. The result was not just a look of thin lips but also the creation of lines of worry radiating to her chin and forecheeks. Her eyes of pale blue were widely open and deep, not appearing in strain but in fatigue. The feel was that she had seen far more of life than she would have wished to and could not imagine a sight of relief. Her soft brown wispy hair was short and combed back from her broad Deutsch forehead with only slight eyebrows arched over the welling eyes. The door to Lamb's bedroom where she stood looking out the window was closed. She did not like her husband, Lemuel, to know she had been sobbing. Her life these past days were chained in regret. Her daughter and only child was a girl fallen from grace and lost to sin. And the man who had gotten her into trouble still was running free in the night.

Anna's dress was always modest with stiff upright blouse collar to her chin and covering her neck, and her skirts reached below her ankles to defy view of all but the soles of her high-buttoned shoes, and then in back, her skirt was uncomfortably thrust out by the large bustle extension. Her physical charms were not for spectacle and distorted beyond imagination. Much of her dress was hidden including the corset held in place by suspenders and petticoats close fitting in front and flared and flounced in the back. Anna was the matron of the house and kept up the appearance even though it was a tomb in the absence of her daughter.

She had taught her lovely daughter, Lamb, to dress modestly also and without attempt to attract lascivious eyes. She would have had her daughter live modestly too but failed as a mother. Anna was a tormented woman these days, one whose life was mired in the past and ruined by events.

Anna was alerted by the alarm at the back door. Who was it who was knocking? Was it Lamb, her daughter, condemned as an unwed mother, come home? No, it was not. It was the neighbor boy, Michael Sipe, knocking at the door. She would let her husband, Lemuel, answer and take care of whatever business the neighbor had.

Anna would get back to her work, trying to forget that her daughter, Lamb, had become pregnant and had no doubt borne an illegitimate child by now, abandoning the way of the Lord. Surely the pregnancy could not have been Lamb's fault! Didn't she wish to live righteously? Hadn't Anna taught her daughter to walk in the way of the spotless and innocent Lamb for whom she was named.

Anna had much work to do. She spent most of her days these days, and since her daughter had left home for God-knows-where, in Lamb's room getting it ready for Lamb's return home. Since there had been such a delay now, Anna had even started getting the arrangements made for the baby.

Soon the girl would return home. There was only the one condition Anna had made of her daughter for her return. She must tell Anna the name of the perpetrator of her downfall. With only the name, whispered softly or written on a scrap of paper, Lamb might resume her life in her family. Then, this one who had raped her would be behind bars. Anna herself would see to it. She would avenge the dishonor of her daughter no matter if it meant her own life. Doesn't God answer a mother's prayers? She prayed to God each day and often that the boy who had caused her daughter's fall from grace would be punished horribly. She wished him cast down into hell in a fiery comet of judgment where Satan himself had been bound for causing sin to wrack the world. Each day of wait must mean the criminal would burn in hell the longer. By the door to her violated daughter's room was the shotgun she carried with her these days to protect herself from the same rape that must have ruined her daughter. Her finger itched to pull its trigger on the one who took from her the innocent child she had borne.

What a surprise it would be for Lamb to see her room changed so. Lamb would come back to a glorious return. She would be so happy! Anna liked to think about that as she busied herself with this little improvement and that as she had done each day since the blowup when Lamb had left.

Now when Lamb returned she would also find everything accommodating even for her child. Was it a boy or a girl? She often wondered about that. Sometimes she did her work for the child thinking it a boy and sometimes as a girl. But lately as she had purchased a ceramic doll's head at Hart and Thayer's Dry Goods House on Main Street in Greenfield for her to turn into a doll, she had hoped and bet on the child being a little girl. Every day her sewing now was devoted to a doll's bonnet or cloak or dress for her new granddaughter made out of scraps or an old dress she could spare for this day's work or that.

Anna had brought in the cradle that she had used to rock Lamb to sleep in before her trouble and had arranged and rearranged baby clothing and toys, finding ever better spots for them to be placed.

When would the world become right again? When could it be that full justice would be done?

Yes, Lamb would return and tell her mother who the father was any day now. Until then, Anna would continue to get Lamb's and the baby's room ready. Surely it would be soon now. After all, Lamb had left in the cold of January and it was now June.

After Michael Sipe left, Anna's husband Lemuel went to Lamb's room where Anna Hackleman was busy with her mother's work.

He stood in the doorway. Anna saw him there and stopped her doings and then rushed to him and asked him to hold her close. The sight of her husband was always a relief to her and the source of what strength she still had. She had always considered him such a handsome catch although by now age was tolling.

Lemuel's hair was prematurely white, a hereditary condition which had begun having its effect when he was barely 40, several years previous. It was neatly parted in its center. He had the friendly look that comes with a face that is handsome, composed and without blemish, but the expression was downcast now, not its usual friendliness upon encounter. His eyes, set deeply in his fair skinned face, were usually narrowly set and attentive to what was before him.

"It was Michael Sipe," Lemuel told his wife. "They have found a body in the river and wanted to know if we might know who it could be."

For a moment Anna's heart fluttered. "Oh, God, it was not the body of a girl was it? Could it have been Lamb?" For a moment the thought floated horribly in her mind that perhaps it might be better if it was Lamb, dead, rather than alive in unwed motherhood. Anna knew this thought was wrong and she wished she could discard it, but it was a bird whose song might have provided some relief. It quickly flew away.

"Oh no," Lemuel told her. "It was a man all right."

Then he continued softly, "Anna you must get over this tragedy of our daughter. Surely by now you must realize she is not coming home. Her love for the father, whoever he might be, is so strong that she will never betray him as her lover. You have attached a condition to our love of her, and love can have no conditions." Anna released herself from Lemuel's embrace. She would not listen to what he said.

Lemuel's words fell silent too lost in memory of his last sight of his daughter. How could he adjust to the loss of this daughter. Can one pretend that love does not exist? How could he forget her words in parting, "Mother and I have argued, father. I must go. If I should stay, I would only be a thorn to her. I have let her down and am tarnished, father, not worthy of being her daughter or yours. Think of me kindly once each day. I have been told I must leave this house." Lemuel had wanted to reach for his daughter to learn more of the engagement but shortly after the kitchen door closed with Lamb's sudden departure, Anna came to him. Here she was, wide-eyed and uncomprehending, his wife, Anna, in his arms, rushing in from the parlor, heaving mightily and sobbing into his ear that he must hold her. Love died before his eyes.

"She is pregnant, Lemuel. Lamb is pregnant!" Anna had told him, "and she will not tell me the father. I have told her to leave this home until she can tell me and I can see him in hell and she restored to reputation." Anna also decided immediately, "None of the neighbors are to know of this. I shall not allow our family name to be scandalized."

And then after she had sobbed in Lemuel's arms for the length of the storm of her grief, she broke away. "Did Lamb really leave?" Anna asked as if recovering from too great a shock or awakening from too terrible a dream.

"Yes," Lemuel had told her. "You told her she must and she did."

"But was I not only speaking in anger to find from her the name of the boy?"

"Yes," Lemuel said. "That is what you have told me was said. But you also told me she would not tell you and see the boy brought to wrath."

"Well then she shall soon return," Anna said matter of factly. "In fact, "I shall go down to the road and await her. She will soon come back and inform us of her assailant so that we can have the boy brought to justice for his crime and then life will resume its course."

There was no stopping Anna as she had followed the same path down to the road that Lamb had followed the several minutes before.

Anna would seat herself at the roadway as the daylight faded. Anna you peer this way and that! Do you feel that Lamb will return to you, Anna! Lamb does not return, Anna!

And now the fingers of the black night begin to clutch at the land. Go inside, Anna. Lamb is not coming back!

But Anna would not give up her post to such a scurrilous force as the night.

There, there it was up in the sky: the North Star! How she hung to the vision of this star and found comfort in its light and twinkle. Even in the blackness of the night there it stood, a sentinel and sign of God's unchanging order. Always the North Star was the same. The law of righteousness did not change either. One might fall in love but never outside of marriage. Always this star beaconed the way to God, never changing from day to day, season to season. All other stars seemed so faded and uncertain in comparison, unprincipled and loose. The righteous do not stray but remain as the North Star affixed in God's order.

Her mind drifted to thoughts of the boy who had brought her daughter to ruin. Let the rest of the blackness hide this man! She would concentrate on the North Star. Let the criminal know the ways of the night. He was its creature, a runner from the light of day, casting about into night secrets, hiding from the truth of righteousness. He should remember that he cannot run from God's order over the world. The North Star would shine down on him too even in the sable night.

And as surely as the North Star would ever prove God steadfast to the righteous, she would meet this boy who had ruined her daughter. She would meet him face to face. No matter that he might attempt concealment in the blackness. She would find him certainly and destroy him. She would dance on his grave and sing hymns that justice prevails.

She again settled herself down. Yes, God would give her this satisfaction. Had a passing cloud hidden the North Star? No, here it came again from the flying clouds. The North Star would never stray from its purpose and course. Anna would not either. She would have this boy pay the price of his sin.

Up above in the heavens, she noted a falling star. It was an omen of someone's fall. An angel was being cast out of heaven into hell in vindication of God's order. It seemed to make a path toward her and burst overhead. Anna smiled, finding comfort in thinking that this would soon be the fate of the boy who had gotten Lamb in trouble.

Much, much later Anna would fall asleep in this place of lookout.

Long past midnight, Lemuel came down the lane to retrieve the failed sentry. Lemuel picked her up and carried her back down the lane to the Hackleman home.

Anna opened her eyes, "Lemuel," she said, "I have prayed that God give me no rest until Lamb returns and her violator is punished horribly. I wish no rest and I will acknowledge no peace until the boy is dead. I shall never yield!"

The saddened man followed Anna's wishes that she stay in Lamb's room for the rest of the night, to be present when Lamb returned.

But that day was long in the past now.

That event, when Lamb had gone, was now distant not by days but by months. Every passing day had remained a weight on Anna's unyielding mind that could not be lifted or cast away.

Lemuel's life, like his wife's, had been one of a grief so deep it could not be spoken. He had left his wife in Lamb's room that night when Lamb had left. Nothing he could say would make any difference or cause Anna to come away.

As Anna had seen her husband leave the room, Anna raised her finger and shook it in a gesture of intensity that dared Lemuel and warned him not to disagree. "She will come back to us, Lemuel, and then we will have the boy in jail and torment as he has caused us! If necessary I will kill him myself!" she said.

The door closed. Lemuel had only looked at her with sympathy for he feared otherwise. Lamb was not going to come home.

Now rest awhile, Anna. Lie down in your absent daughter's bed. This place of comfort and rest is not foreign to you. Often over the years you lay down here with Lamb as a child cradled in your arm, in former days when she was young and innocent. Remember the nights when she could not sleep and needed her mother to be with her? Here you warded off the terrors of the black nights telling her tales to spin her into sleep. You sang her the old songs of the elders that you had learned as a child to calm her and convince her that the world was a place of peace and content. Remember if you will, Anna, how convincing you were when you told her to never worry for you would always keep her warm and safe. Under the bed still rests your grandmother's prayer book, Christliche Betractungen, gathering dust. Remember the prayers you had Lamb repeat from it with you and how you wished Lamb to have this leathery volume as an inheritance except that you demanded she leave the home before she could take with her a single thing?

Lemuel felt paralyzed. Why was his wife so deluded? How could Anna believe their lives could return to the way they had been before? It was an outrage to think Anna did not know her own daughter's heart. Surely, she knew her daughter. She should know her daughter. It takes time to know any person and a mother who has looked into her daughter's eyes as a baby and in each step of growth has the time to come to know this person bonded not just in observation but in the heart.

Lamb was not to see her lover persecuted! Why could not Anna remember the first flush of their own love when Lemuel could feel his spirit fly to heaven and circle him overhead constantly like a hungry and predatious hawk demanding to dive to earth? Could she not remember how reckless is youthful love?

Lemuel wished he could return to his daughter's room and try to convince his hysterical little Deutsch farmwife that you cannot make a heart betray somebody. You can require but it will not listen. Lemuel knew his daughter was as stubborn as his wife on things that were important to her. If she had decided she would never see her lover persecuted, no threat or demand by either her mother or him or both could change her mind.

And outside, on this much later day, Michael Sipe had mounted his horse. Not for his hearing was a nearby meadowlark chut chut chutting the joy of the summer season so many months now after Lamb's departure from the Hackleman farm and his life. Michael snapped the reins and went riding down the lane of the Hackleman home, his long light brown hair floating behind in the soft June winds, toward the trace through the busy Deutschlands of Hancock County and Central Indiana, an empty place to him where there was no cheer.

You might well notice the set of his chin, strongly jutted out as against fate. But do not look at the eyes. Those eyes are not focused upon the land or its present time. They are lost in the recollection and image of a young girl for whom his heart beat yet and for whom the days outside of her love were as lived in a desert from which life has fled.

9

Lemuel's Discovery

Out in a rural Central Indiana cropfield a great steam engine was belching its plumes of smoke in blobby black puffs from the stack over its huge boiling cylinder. By its side, the men of the threshing machine crew were busy at their tasks, sweating, strange sights in tanned faces hidden under low-brimmed felt hats, long-sleeved checked and plaid shirts over their muscular arms and heaving chests, tails out, cut by the lines of suspenders over trousers from which boots dug into the clods. This was the look of a crew harvesting wheat with the new steam engine threshers of the 1890s.

Otherwise, the July day was bright with blue sky when John Pritchard, who worked for the Greenfield Paper Mill, came by the Hackleman place. Only wispy clouds sheltered the dry Hancock County land from the sun's rays where the harvesting of the Hackleman's wheat was underway.

Such a blue sky over the land of the Hoosiers! It was the same sky sheltering Lamb Hackleman, the shamed and sinful daughter, already at work at the paper mill, as it did her mother, busy in the farmhouse kitchen, her father, Lemuel, working with the harvesting crew, Michael Sipe, cultivating the farm field next to that of the Hackleman farm behind his team of restless horses making slow passes in lethargic recollection of his better days, and, somewhere, the Wild Bull of Blue River, terrorizing the land. All breathed the same nourishing air.

The time was mid-July, 1894, and the field was Lemuel Hackleman's. The season had arrived for Lemuel to harvest the wheat he had drilled along the level county trace to the far west of the Hackleman farm. The golden wheat was ready and waiting with its grains waving heavily into the warm air. Lemuel had engaged a threshing crew to snatch the moment.

The Scott Brothers owned the monster steam engine and although it could be moved on its own wide wheels, flat and spiked, they pulled it instead to the neighbor farms with a team of mules that were now down at Dilly Crick tied to a corkscrew willow in its shady woods. Using the mules to transport the machine between farms avoided the possibility of overuse or breakdown of the fragile machine. Now the thresher was at its work traversing the field, separating the wheat heads from its straw.

Lemuel had pride in this year's stand of wheat and pride in the progress that Hoosier agriculture had made since the days when his father, Abraham Hackleman, had sewn his wheat and oats on these same fields by hand and harvested his crops with a wooden cradle at first and then a reaper as the century progressed, and on to a horse-drawn self- binder. This elder Hackleman would never have dreamed that a steam engine might provide the power to harvest wheat! Abraham would have known content from his son's crop this year and how he was giving new life to the land.

But a stranger had come by this morning to drink in the scene. John Pritchard walked his horse to a stop and evaluated the sight as he had so many others like it this season. After the wheatheads were removed, this field was being littered with exactly what he wanted - straw. Yes, this straw would be just what the doctor ordered. Then, satisfied with this conclusion, John Pritchard focused on the men he saw busy around the belching steam engine. He was trying to make out which of the crew might be the owner of the farm. He craned his neck in this direction and another. Then he picked out one who seemed to stand more to the side, Lemuel, in fact the only face among the five there at work he had not seen before on this kind of enterprise. He would go see this man.

John Pritchard was a field man for the Weston Paper Manufacturing Company, Greenfield's paper mill, and it was said he could smell out straw for his paper mill to buy. His boast was that there wasn't a single farmer at work bundling small grain, a horse treading around a grain separator or a steam engine for threshing that he didn't know about in all of Hancock County or the Hoosier Deutschlands of the Blue River.

Now as Lemuel Hackleman was harvesting his wheat, John Pritchard went to talk to him, an oddly ill-fitting looking person for the scene wearing the latest fashion, a covert checked coat with velvet collar and the modern twill trousers, the kind with wide legs that flared from the knees on down sometimes called "spring bottoms." His small eyes, nervous and flighty manner, keyed him as a highly intense individual indeed. But he cut quite an impressive figure and made a point of it too! He was from town and civilization, a different place from the habitats of these country bumpkins.

John walked gingerly through the field so that the straw did not scratch his spats. When he got to Lemuel, he sized up the farmer he saw before him, tipped his bowler hat with its curly brim, and extended his hand for a shake, introducing himself as a man whom Lemuel had waited his lifetime to meet.

Lemuel stood beside him as a huge man to a boy. Lemuel was a big man, nearly 6 foot and heavy of chest and with thinner tapering limbs and legs that did not quite match his heaviness and bulk. His jaw was set on a rectangular face except for its lower lines containing his mouth that rather appeared as a thin "m." The farmer cut an imposing figure and he was a man well respected too for his savvy and "horse sense" as well as being considered a very strong and hard working fellow.

"Interested in some more money for your crops?" John Pritchard asked Lemuel.

Lemuel stuck his hands together behind his back, the way he did when listening, and began his "talked to" sway back and forth after their handshake.

Well, it was true what the man was saying. Seventy cents a bushel wasn't so much for his wheat, soft red wheat and not so hard as the best for flour... especially when he could make some more money than that. But sell his wheat straw to make paper? Lemuel had not even dreamed of such a thing. The new paper mill in Greenfield was buying straw to make paper out of. Well, well! Sure he had heard that the Gas Boom in the county was bringing all sorts of new industries to town, but this?

"We'll buy your straw and give you top dollar!" John Pritchard told him with a draw of his mouth and reassuring nod of his head. "Here's my card. Just bunch this straw up and load it and you're looking at some real money here."

To Lemuel the deal sounded pretty good. Straw didn't have much use. Most of it not bundled for stock bedding was left in the fields. Of course the price wasn't what it was for hay, or timothy, or even prairie hay that a farmer could use for winter stalk feed. But then $4 a ton was more like a gift anyway!

After the smooth talker left the Hackleman farm, Lemuel thought about it some and decided he would take a load into the paper mill on one of the very next few days to see about this.

Why not. Any chore was a blessing these days, any work to get his mind off the disappearance of his daughter, Lamb, from his life.

Lemuel was not a complicated man. He had simply lived to love those persons and things he was close to. You would include in this circle his little wife, Anna, of course. He loved her with all of his heart. But you would also include his farm and all he attended to on the farm, his crops, his sparse machinery, his farm animals, and even the air that seemed so heavy with exuberant growth this year. And yet, the daughter, his only child, Lamb, was not in the circle of his love any longer. She was gone and he didn't know how to love her any more now that she was no longer close to him. This was the great frustration of his life. How do you love someone you are separated from? All you want to do is have them back to hug and look at and hold so tightly that they can never leave you alone again.

He tried to forget that Lamb had always been a chick beneath his wing, but he could not. Her presence on the farm had always seemed a source of great energy. He loved doing things because it was for his progeny. The thought of her had moved him to clear the far fields so that her generation might have more than his had. She had been with him as a child, playing in or near the cropfields, and Lamb knew the farm and the Blue River lands, its secret places and wet backlands, as did no one more than himself. Perhaps only the Wild Bull he could so often hear would know so well-this land- as he and his daughter. How he missed having his daughter with him at harvest time. How she would have loved to see the black plumes from the threshing machine cylinder and hear the steam engine hiss and chug as it pulled the threshing equipment behind it!

This prior night, as those of late, he had prayed, kneeling by his bed, his silent prayer for knowledge of Lamb's whereabouts. The worry about where she was seemed to drive him into exhaustion far more deadening than did his daily toiling. Could not this frustration at least end? What had happened to his daughter still as pure to him as an angel? Could she not return home under some guise of heaven and be his pride and joy once again?

Sun rays were yet spearing the rosy horizon this morning, two mornings later, when Lemuel hitched his field team of horses to the wagon of wheat straw he had loaded up as high as he could, tucking its stalks under a canvas and tying it down with rope. This would be the morning when Lemuel would drive his wagon filled with straw down the lane from his barn to the trace that led over to the Range Line and then north to the rutty and thinly graveled National Road to Greenfield and its new paper mill.

Then, close to an hour later, as the morning cleared the haze from the sky, up ahead was Greenfield. Lemuel had reached the heights to the east of town before the land began its dip down to the bank of the Brandywine Crick, cutting from the north to the south, another tributary of the Blue River. From these heights the entire scene of the Hoosier country to the west could be scoped. Greenfield, the county seat of the Hoosier County of Hancock, lay before him.

One would hardly know what to expect seeing these days as you came to Greenfield and saw it from here. Change was rampant. The place looked like a huge construction site. Natural gas derricks shot up from tree clearings everywhere. From one day to the next, the sight would hardly look the same.

Where was the little village, the county seat, the Greenfield he had seen so often over the years, so like a small crowd of wooden frame buildings in a row along the National Road, in its center a simple two-story courthouse already torn down? The place had been so insignificant that the greening trees would almost hide its entirety from spring to fall.

This place he was seeing was not as before!

Scattered across the horizon were the brick buildings of a profusion of factories in multiple wide clearings from which came the sounds of grinding machinery and heavy and light industry. It seemed like every month saw at least one new industry arrive in this place. Here a nail factory. There a window glass plant. Over there a company manufacturing the fashionable new adjustable chairs being so highly advertised all over the country. The world had beaten a path here to the Hoosier state as businessmen considered the bounty of free inexhaustible gas and free lands ready for industrial plucking. Here was the start of a new world fuel by nauseating gas. The smells were not the only indicia. There were sounds too, especially of the trains along the Panhandle rail line which screeched into the air at least hourly. Greenfield was the only Gas Boom town along its line in Indiana. Richmond, Columbus and Pittsburgh were to its east and Indianapolis to its west. Here in Greenfield, before Lemuel's eyes, was the start of a new world in which Midwestern American industry would bloom and change the world from an economy of family farm life to something new. What would it lead to?

Then too, huge homes were being built, not just of flimsy frame, but brick houses in multiple stories, with towered roofs, porches at surprising levels, stained glass windows, gingerbread and trim of strange and excessive proportions.

Towering high into the air of the county seat, as would the hugest castle of the Palatinate, was the new courthouse, rising in monumental limestone block after limestone block, forming itself into fantastic towers and rounded parapets. There was BOOM spelled loudly in many other construction projects visible as well. Money, lots of it, was here to be spent. Lavish spending was obvious everywhere. The newly discovered natural gas domes underneath this land of bounty would provide fuel forever!

All was new and appeared bustling, even the miserable rows of workers' homes and shanties which Lemuel began passing as he struck at his team to reach the Morristown Pike entry into the paper mill.

He had heard the rumors about this workers' camp and the people who had been drawn to Greenfield to work in the new factories who lived in it. It was Oklahoma and contained wretched workers who were paid wages scarcely above the level of subsistence. Some were saying that Oklahoma was a fact that the county must live with. Many manufacturers and industrialists were moving factories to Indiana not only because of the Gas Boom but because the East was unionizing and this movement had not reached the hinterlands. Here in Greenfield, companies could hire labor dirt cheap and need not worry about such potential horrors as labor demands for shorter work weeks or minimum wages on threat of strikes.

At the pike, Lemuel turned his team into the array of enormous new brick buildings composing the Weston Paper Manufacturing Company, the largest paper mill of its type in all the world. As he wound his wagon down the dusty road, he passed by its central tall vertical digester building where the caustic acids soaked and broke down the straw fibers. Here was where straw was selected for feeding for a "cook." The smell of the area so close to the black liquor fluid of the digester was caustic and hurt his nose. Surely an acid odor such as this must not be so concentrated!

The mill girls were out in front, dressed in their long dresses covered by leather aprons that not only touched the ground in front but which arose from their waistlines to be tied around the neck. The girls were scarcely recognizable as they were bent over the straw, bundling it into bunches feedable to the digester. Their hands were encased in leather gloves too and straw bonnets were drawn over their heads shading and rendering them anonymous. Lemuel's attention was drawn to the gloves of one of the girls. The stitching was undone and the red of drawing blood was staining its rear side over raw flesh.

A supervisor was standing nearby, leaning against the building. He was middle-aged, named Gustavus Crider, and without apron over his checked trousers and high buttoned shirt with waistcoat. He was shouting through massive beard at the girls who would look up at him from their bendings to sort and bundle the straw with looks like, "Sir, we are doing all that we can!" No actual response however came from the girls. Chattering and idle talk were apparently forbidden.

And yet one of these sweating girls, Yes, even this girl with the torn glove, looked so recognizable to Lemuel that he was forced to take a double-take, and then a triple. This girl, one of these weary girls at the back-breaking labor, was his beautiful daughter Lamb gone so long from his home! How could she be here? Had she had her baby? Where was his grandchild? All these questions buzzed at him like a swarm of bees.

When Lemuel first recognized his daughter, so long disappeared, then pregnant but refusing to name the father and cause of her downfall, the instant in time demanded he run to her, to hold her in his arms, to listen to the music of her voice, to ask all of the hidden questions that had been welling in his heart. Had she given birth to his grandchild? If so, could he see the baby? Here was the little girl still a teenager whose life he had given wing.

Lemuel did not, however, act on impulse. It was not his way. So, that instant of time when he would have rushed to his daughter had passed quickly and the dampening reality of his life closed in on him like a vise slowly squeezing away his joy of discovery of his daughter's whereabouts. He did not know what to do. This was after all the child who had been told she must leave his farm. Lemuel had his wife, Anna, to think about too. She would not approve of his contact with her daughter short of Lamb's returning to the farm, confessing her sin, and cooperating in the punishment of the boy responsible for her unwed pregnancy. Lemuel could not help but shudder at the alternative to Anna's demand that Lamb had taken. She had begun a new life at such a price! But he saw no wrong in what she was doing. Her work was hard but honest labor! Lamb had simply purchased her freedom from shame by escape into the life of a mill girl at Greenfield's paper mill. Such a different life she was now leading than the one she had known on her farm home. No doubt she was raising the baby, if the pregnancy had resulted in a birth, on her pittance wage.

Anna would have killed him for even thinking it, but Lemuel felt pride in seeing Lamb where she was, at labor. He too had known its satisfactions, those that the young learn only through maturity. Perhaps he should leave well enough alone. How hard it was to decide! Interference in Lamb's life was perhaps not for him to undertake! What good would it do to bring up the acrimony of the past? Lemuel knew Anna's demands would never be agreed to. Lamb would never see the man who got her in trouble brought to justice! Lemuel had known that from the look on his daughter's face as she left. Her stubbornness was a moat between his wife and daughter. Their alienation was beyond his fixing. He could not go to Lamb.

Lemuel's prayers were answered just knowing where Lamb was. He could ask no more. Now, having cut her off from the support of his home, he was entitled only to live in the shadow of her life. He had forfeited his right as a father by siding with the tragic girl's mother who had made the demand that Lamb could never return home until the man who caused her pregnancy be punished horribly. What else could Lemuel do? What else could he do? And yet his love of this child remained burning in his heart.

He must cautiously navigate the shoals of this discovery. He would not have her run further away for all the world perhaps to a place where he might never see her again.

Lemuel hurried his team of horses pulling his wagon load of straw past the scene of the mill girls, and his daughter, Lamb, hard at work sorting and bundling straw, then joined a line of about 20 other wagons up ahead. This was the busiest time yet for the purchasing season for the mill, the short days after the wheat harvest. Most of the purchases would have to be effected quickly and then the produce would have to be stored in the elevator building across the lane from the purchasing office.

The line of wagons inched along to the platform scales up ahead in front of the purchasing office. The seller drove his team through the scales so that the wagon was situated on the wooden platform of the scales and then to the unloading area where the straw was removed by a rough looking bunch of boys with pitchforks. Inside a shack beside the platform scales, the weight of the wagon was noted by a purchasing clerk and the wagon would later be re-weighed without the straw after its unloading. The difference would be the amount of straw sold for which the farmer would receive his pay.

As Lemuel arrived for his turn at unloading, the men lazily leaning against storage elevator steps were called to their duty, and they came to his wagon at the time for unloading and gave him a greeting.

"Say," he asked one of them, "is one of those mill girls a girl named Lamb?"

"Oh, yes," came the reply and the finest one of them, too. She lives over at Oklahoma with a family," he added. "Her life is left at that! She don't come around or see nobody."

As the boy started to leave, Lemuel could not leave the information at that. He grabbed at the boy's shirt, a move that startled the young man and he shook off the tug.

"And where in Oklahoma does she live?" Lemuel asked.

The boy looked at the old man doubtfully. What business was it of his? Then seeing the old man looking harmless and only inquisitive and not a menace, he told that the girl was said to live with a family named the Ferrees...on the third street north in Oklahoma...the only house with porch front and back...though if it were true he would not know.

After Lemuel's second trip on the scales, this time empty, he went inside the purchase shack where the agent had figured the tonnage of his straw and prepared a transaction payment. Lemuel's sale of his straw was effected. He was paid inside the office by the purchasing clerk, a little man wearing the fashionable droopy mustache of the 1890s. The man's face seemed so fleshy and his eyes so sunken within the flesh. Here it was summer, and yet the man - was it to impress the country bumpkins like Lemuel - wore a high buttoned three- piece suit, unbuttoned so that his fancy gold watch on a chain could be seen pocketed in the suit's waistcoat. Lemuel, dressed much less formally, was handed a check. He was not a noticing mood about anyone's appearance. How could he care about the businessman's appearance anyway, now that he had found his daughter?

A check! Lemuel handled it gingerly in his hand, as if were hot, and then drew it close to his eyes for a gander. What good was a check! This piece of rectangular paper was the first one of these things he had ever received. He had never even seen a check before. Lemuel had always traded for money. There was hardly anything to it- this check. Across the top in a huge black box was the name Weston Paper Company. But not just this. From the bottom of this rectangle emerged curlycues of lines and bars with circles that ran to the edge, patterned into boxes with designs topped by palm leaves and configured within a circle of geometric design that turned the W of Weston into something haloed. It certainly looked fancy enough to be something of value. Then underneath it said, Greenfield, Ind. with a blank in which the date had been filled in and a line ("Pay to the order of...") on which the name Lemuel Hackleman had been scripted in. The amount of the sale and the signature of the purchasing agent were affixed. In the lower left corner was the address: To Greenfield Banking Co.

"It's as good as money!" the purchasing agent said seeing Lemuel look at it so dubiously. Few of the Deutschmen who came to the mill for the first time had ever seen a check and he was used to their amazement. So, noticing Lemuel's strange look and doubtful scrunch of his face, the man added, "You can take it to the bank if you want to and get the cash out of it." To Lemuel this sounded like a pretty good idea. Besides that he had a use for the money from the check anyway.

Only one more question he had of the man, and this one a question he had feared to address with the scales boy. "Do you know of the mill girl, Lamb Hackleman?" Lemuel asked.

"Oh, yes," the purchasing clerk said.

"And does she have a child?"

"We must not talk of such things," the Clerk said. "This mill hires no employees who are of ill reputation. Mr. Rock, the owner's representative, would never allow such a thing! Girls of loose morals are not hired here, no!"

But as Lemuel left, the clerk came around the counter to draw Lemuel closer. "Do I recollect from the name I placed on the check that you are a relative?" The clerk had recalled the name Hackleman, as Lamb's last name, was the one he had penned on the check.

"Yes," Lemuel readily admitted, not adding that he was her father.

"Well, it is said that she does have a child. Some say so, but of course I do not know of it," he added stiffly.

"Oh, thank you!" Lemuel said to the man, losing all reserve with the news and hugging the surprised man in his arms before leaving.

Lemuel step had now a spring. Soon he drove his team of horses by the building where Lamb had gone inside. Lemuel could detect no trace of her, not even a sound. At this stage of the milling cycle, there came forth from the mill buildings only the rumbling noise of the steam boilers boiling the soda out of the black liquor, punctuated with the huge slurps of the nauseous liquid pouring through clanking feeding pipes from the pounding re-circulating pumps.

Lemuel drove his team from the premises and soon reached the National Road, but instead of taking its turn back toward his home in the country, he drove west toward the town of Greenfield, finding himself in busier traffic. He waited his turn to take the bridge over the Brandywine Crick. This bridge spanned the stream under a single arch of iron over what might have been 50 or 60 feet of expanse. It took only one team at a time. The iron arch was buried at each end in huge stone embankments extending twenty feet or so onto the banks. Supporting beams from this arch held up the structure of the wooden planking but Lemuel's horses still made a clatter and a rumbling as they pulled the wagon across and ascended the gradual meadow-like rise that would lead to the center of the Gas Booming town. Greenfield, beyond, had doubled, tripled, and then quadrupled in size in the last handful of years. Huge homes were being built on either side of the road. The sounds were of the humming and grinding of the many new factories. Near each was a huge derrick poking into the sky. Each derrick marked a site for tapping natural gas.

On the streets of Greenfield were the vehicles of every commerce. Horses and people were in an almost equal proportion. Traffic was borne on open produce wagons, pulled by variously colored horses in high wooden collars or closed marketing wagons painted in colors with an occasional advertisement displayed. Here would come a buggy pulled by a single snorting horse in the bobbing forward movement that horses have when at an in-town walk. Many sidewalks were filled too with pedestrians. Since it was day, the ladies, some with parasols as protection from the sun, were in the downtown - a place they would never go at night. No longer were the pigs and cattle allowed upon these main thoroughfares now that Greenfield had come of age and had entered into the world's consciousness as an industrial and manufacturing boom area. Marks of this new age were everywhere. Virtually the entire downtown area, especially the more imposing buildings around the Courthouse, were of new construction and not just locally manufactured brick, but also there were buildings of Bedford limestone, some with carved or poured mouldings imported into the area over the busy Panhandle railroad line from the construction material houses of the East. The downtown also had its own odor, that of natural gas, which could not be escaped. The ornate street lights along the downtown streets were flambeaus and burned as flares during the night and even until daylight and the odor of the gas clung and stayed during the daylight hours beyond freshening.

Lemuel had been directed to go to one of the new banks, this one the Greenfield Banking Company, chartered 1871 after the collapse of Indiana's state-run Bank of Indiana. Lemuel knew it was across the street from the Courthouse and its description.

Such an imposing structure was this Greenfield Banking Company of the 1890s! How could one even enter it, it looked so imposing. Barely 25 feet of frontage between two other buildings was squeezed into huge arched spaces with fluted flat columns surmounted by ornate scrollwork. Over these 10-foot-high arches were limestone curtains draped - each one gathered over one of the four arched spaces by an iron star. The facade of the second floor was equally ornate and cluttered except that the columns were not fluted but carved as lotus stems upon whose stylized blooms began the shelter of the roof. Within the dark first-floor spaces were shadowy windows apparently not intended to allow light to enter because the windows were closed with black shutters with the exception of the shadowy space of a doorway in the westernmost of the arched spaces offering entry up a flight of limestone stairs. Lemuel climbed these stairs, entering the bank. There at a teller's cage, he cashed the check he had been given for his straw

Now he would go and give the money to his grandchild before he returned to the country. He stopped to turn into the workers' camp of Oklahoma. Not much later, he found the home with porch front and back, the residence of the Ferrees.

Lemuel left his wagon to confront the man observing him seated on the front porch of the home. Adam Ferree sat straight-backed on the porch of the home, elbows on thighs, his arms and his thick hands dangling between his knees, his useless smashed feet concealed in boots. He did not stand up at the approach of the strange man. Adam could not get around easily even to get up from where he was sitting. His huge bulk of chest gave the impression the man was fat, so fat he could hardly hold his girth within the vest tightly buttoned so as to crease ludicrously from the strain. His face too was rather chubby too and with very marked features, nothing smooth or youthful. Was he in his fifties? It would so appear for his mustache and goatee were white around his mouth but still dark brown at the chin.

As Lemuel approached closer, Adam Ferree maintained the set to his face, the look of a careful scrutinizing man who had seen much of the world and bore more than his portion of its sorrows. Adam did not particularly welcome visitors, any one of whom might be a bill collector.

Lemuel realized immediately that before him must be the baby-sitter for his grandson while his daughter, Lamb, was at work during the light hours at the paper mill.

What could Lemuel say? How could he approach the man who was doing what he would himself do if God had given him the grace? Would he take the money from the sale of the straw?

Lemuel came forward and introduced himself. The meeting did not go well. The man's eyes retained their scrutiny of Lemuel and their caution as to his intentions. So, this was the grandfather of the baby! How could he know that! Lamb had said nothing to the Ferrees about the appearance of her parents.

Even while Lemuel said "Hello," there came a crack in the door and the man's wife came out, she who, along with the man, had taken in Lamb when her family had released her to face the shame of unwed pregnancy alone out in the world. The woman's face was hidden under a straw bonnet held in place under her chin with a yellow ribbon. She was of about the same stature as her husband except you would call her stout rather than heavy or even plump. She wore a clean blouse with ruffle at the waist and a long skirt of simple material gathered at the waist. Her look was really rather blank, eyes affixed on Lemuel but not staring. There was no expression, no expectation in her drawn mouth that she would respond to speech. Her eyes, like those of her husband, were marked with attentiveness to what Lemuel would say but with cautious concern. These two were the guardians and care givers to the illegitimate child of his daughter's sin.

And yet they seemed as guardian angels to Lemuel who could really find no words to speak in justification of his presence there.

All he could say was that he wished to see the child of Lamb Hackleman if they should be so kind as to permit it. After a glance between themselves the man and his wife gave their consent. They would not challenge this man's claim to be a grandfather. Lemuel seemed no threat. The two good folk took Lemuel inside their home to the corner where, on the cot of Lamb's renting, the box crate was bearing the child.

"She settled to call his name, Pleasant," the man said, adding, "He don't have a last name."

There he was, Lamb's baby and his very own grandson, sleeping in a world he could not fathom, his head at an awkward angle nestled there in a simple blanket. Where were his eyes? Hidden behind heavy lids closed in sleep. Lemuel reached down to try to analyze what he was seeing and measured him involuntarily, finding him roughly two of his huge calloused hands down and one across. Then the stiff fingers touched the head with its fuzziness hardly covering the soft float of pink skin, stopping only to blink at the strange wrinkles of the baby's ears. Everything was there for this little grandson of his, but everything was so very miniature. Fingers, toes? He had them all. Should he wake up the child and introduce himself as his grandpa? A touch of his cheek did not cause the slumbering child to open his eyes. No, the eyes, seeing some peace that adults do not, were busy viewing another shore.

"Do you want to hold him?" the lame man asked.

Lemuel did indeed! He reached down to raise the child to his chest. The child was too light! The baby was hardly graspable, a fairy of bulk without weight. Even so breath came and went from the tiniest flaring nose that he could have ever imagined. And its mouth opened, pursed and closed, making successive efforts at expressions, telescoping all of them, in practice for later use. So this had been the child that his daughter, Lamb, had carried so uncomfortably and with a singleness of purpose - the child's welfare. There was no blemish, no labeling of sin, no illegitimacy and no downcasting possible to this life force in bloom and flow. Here would be the place to which the

winged hopes of his every future prayer would be sent so swiftly.

At his departure, Lemuel offered the money he had earned for his straw. The eyes of the husband and wife met and silently agreed. "No," the man said. "We think it best not to accept the money you offer. Lamb's wages pay her fare and that of the child. We ourselves accept no charity. If your daughter wishes it, you had best find that out from her." The older man, walking gimpily, showed Lemuel to the door of the small home.

"Please do not tell Lamb of this visit," the old man begged. "Promise me! Promise me that!" They did.

Lemuel left the scene with great sadness. It would not be he who God would permit to wage the great battles in the caring for his grandson, but rather these two simple folk whom he had never met before. He must disappear again from the life of his daughter leaving her in strife. "Forgive me, little one," Lemuel choked to himself. "Will you one day forgive me? In recompense, I will hold you forever in my heart and find every new way to love you that God graciously will allow."

No more could the tired grandfather do but return home to Anna. It would be best not to arouse his wife with the news he had learned of Lamb's whereabouts. To do so would be to antagonize fate and further fuel the fire of anger. He could only stand by and watch the two women in his life stubbornly uphold what each felt compelled to do.

10

Wild Bull's Danger

Liberty Trees stepped outside his door this morning, 1894, in the fullness of the morning summer sunshine. Poor old fellow. The sunshine was a shadow to him for he saw stars most of the time. He was an inventor.

He was strange to the ways of the world at the very least. A farmer who always wore a Sunday tie!!! His face seemed hardly human too, more blurry, showing no facial lines or beard, nothing except black looking eyes like little specks of coal and a beak of a nose over a mouth as a line tightly sealed - for he rarely spoke. He also always wore a cap with steel bill that served as a porch roof for his head.

There were a million things that came into his mind for him to do this day. Yes, and he must get busy, because Liberty Trees had every intention of doing them all. His mind worked that way. It is that way with an inventor. That's how he thought of himself even though many of his neighbors would have thought of him as a farmer or perhaps small livestocker on Six Mile Crick. Some would use the word crackpot or crazy.

Liberty Trees was one of the more free- thinking of the men of the Deutsch neighborhood. He prided himself on his inventions. He had sent into the Patent Office more new ideas than Thomas Edison. For example, you could always tell he was coming by his walk. It looked like where he had been. One of his inventions had been shoes that had a heel in front and sole behind. He said they provided safety because no one would follow him since his steps would always lead away.

His passion had been electricity. Out in his barn was the famous generatormobile known throughout the neighborhood. He was working on it a little every day, really one of the first electric cars in the world. He had taken to the theories of electrical induction as a duck takes to water. A huge magnet formed the side structure of the wagon and extended 20 feet into the air. Inside was an equally mammoth thin copper disc that could be turned by a shaft connected to bicycle pedals on the floor of his wagon seat. Liberty Tree's brilliance and genius came from his discovery that bicycle pedaling could power an engine producing electricity, what Michael Faraday had earlier proven could be powered by steam power or water power half a century earlier. The electricity from this arrangement was transformed and caused a gear to turn connected to the rear wagon wheels. Liberty was oblivious to one of the main side effects - a continuous shock that followed every metal piece in the wagon including the pedals he was pushing. He not only didn't seem to mind. In fact, he rather liked it and when he pedaled hard enough he could gage how well he was doing by the shock he was enjoying. When he was pedaling furiously, his generatormobile could outrun any shelled creature in the county.

But his generator didn't have to be so mobile. The shaft on the huge copper disc could be disconnected from the pedals and be run by Lib's team of mules going around a circular run. This day, he would hook up his mules for supplementary power to operate his newest invention - an electric fence. He would see if his electric fence would work. Liberty rigged a pole over each mule's back with a tasty bunch of hay to dangle in front of the mule's mouth just beyond nibble. This would be a little motivation to keep the old trudgers on the go.

Lib would try out for size 6 gauge wire for his fence. A single wire of electricity ought to keep his cattle in and then he wouldn't have to fix that broken down fence. Having his cattle pasture where they were supposed to be took too much of his time from the more pressing inventions he was working on. He hated it when some strange Wild Bull kept jumping into his pasture to visit his heifers without his knowing about it. His problem wasn't unique; many of the farmers were complaining. In fact there were some of his heifers giving birth to little Wild Bulls as were appearing in so many of the other herds of the Blue River neighborhood. Something had to be done or there would be nothing but little Wild Bulls in every pasture.

The coil of wire was easy enough to string around his back pasture. He took it out in the field for installation. Yes, it ought to work. He unspooled the electric wire around the pasture and into the short woods along Six Mile Crick tributary of Blue River. It was only an experiment anyway and would only be for a short time. The next day a stock man was coming to take his cattle to the abattoir, sometimes called a slaughterhouse, for butchering and ridding him of the bother of them anyway. Surely the wire would hold the cattle for one night!

The only problem was a visitor in the herd who Liberty had no idea of. It was the Wild Bull of Blue River.

The Wild Bull began haunting other farms after Lamb had left and his lair in his secret place in the Blue River back country became so lonely. The Wild Bull had shown up at most farms and knew most herds. He also knew how fickle was fate when it came to how the cattle were treated. Some had grassy pastures and clean bedding in spacious barns, and some did not, but were left in small fenced weedy fields all year. Some livestockers oiled the backs of the herds to keep down the flies, some had fly bars, and some did nothing at all about the horn flies and horse flies.

The Wild Bull had come to Liberty's herd for a visit with his particularly coquettish heifers and was not aware that such a thing as butchering the herd the next day was in the offing. Actually, the Wild Bull rather liked Liberty Trees' herd. He had been wandering around the countryside looking for companionship for many days. In the absence of his Lamb, he had kept himself busy on his own project. The Wild Bull had been looking for the perfect livestocker. He would see if this Liberty Trees would be the man.

During the night, the Wild Bull tried to escape the strange wire that Liberty had placed around the field. He treated this weird shocking wire as would a student of geography, as a learning experience of exploring where land features were and where the wire wasn't. But, every time the Wild Bull would think to leave the perimeter through the wire, one of those old mules would want a taste of that dangled hay and start up, sending out a current around Liberty's wire. The Wild Bull disastrously decided to try to wait things out. In fact the Wild Bull was forced to change his generally low opinion of fencing.

Unfortunately, the next morning, the entire herd, including the Wild Bull, was loaded up into stock trailers to be taken to the butcher in Greenfield who ran its abattoir.

Speaking of projects, likewise, for many days, this butcher, too, had one. He had been looking for the perfect beef carcass.

How strange it was that this inventor with his project, the butcher with his project and the Wild Bull with his project should all find their projects intertwined.

After a bumpy ride along the National Road to Greenfield, all of the stock were placed in a pen outside the abattoir along the Brandywine Crick that meandered through Greenfield. The water from this part of Brandywine Crick tasted good, unlike that down below the paper mill where so much of the soda liquor from the mill was getting into the crick.

After stretching his legs, the Wild Bull got his first look at the butcher, a short, stocky, heavily bearded young man whose name was Frank, named after a Frankfurter his mother had particularly enjoyed before his birth. His last name was Schlopfhs (rhymes with chops). Frank also got his look at the Wild Bull. Frank was very appreciative. The Wild Bull looked very interesting, and Frank could see the potential of every visitor to his abattoir. Frank knew beef carcasses very intimately. In fact today was the day when Frank liked to have visitors because it was butchering day for the beef. Twice a week Frank devoted to butchering beef.

Of the rest of the week he butchered hogs one day and packaged both the beef and the pork on the rest. He was busy and ordinarily didn't get to enjoy the finer points of his craft. In a typical week he would butcher between 20 to 40 cattle - enough for the groceries and meat markets in town.

Even though he didn't have lots of leisure, the butcher still took the time to assess each visitor for the qualities of the perfect carcass he would treat with surgical precision in reaching every cut of beef. He spent his life praying for the perfect carcass. This carcass would provide the perfect ribeye. There wasn't a head of beef cattle in the county he had not evaluated for its muscling in relation to its skeletal size. He got hot flushes of hatred whenever he viewed fat thicknesses over the ribeye. One day his search for the perfect carcass would be over.

Although there are many stars in the sky, the night before a good one must have shone down on him because this day Frank felt that he had got his wish to come true. As he looked at the Wild Bull he thought to himself that at last he had found the perfect ribeye steak.

Fate had finally dealt him an ace. He got ready his 22 caliber rifle for the day's work.

The abattoir was divided into two sections. One was a packaging section where the slaughtered cattle and hogs, dressed and cut into portions, were prepared for marketing or home consumption. Beef carcasses are of two types, block beef and processed meats. Block beef is beef that is suitable for sale over the block. This is beef reduced to sides, quarters, wholesale cuts or retail cuts. It is usually kept at a chill at temperatures in the locker freezer room about 34 degrees. If frozen it is kept for several months. Processed meats are the rest of the meat which could be either boned out, made into sausage, ground for canned meat, or sometimes dried for smoking. The locker was a place where the public could visit. Here you would find wire baskets of white paper wrapped meat portions stored in its freezing compartments.

The other section was the place from which the shots rang. It was called the "kill floor". An animal was brought in front of Frank and with 22 caliber rifle raised, loaded, trigger cocked, Frank would aim it at the animal's head, between the eyes, and blast away. The animal would sink and bellow and die.

Was this the fate of the Wild Bull? Was he to become the world's perfect ribeye?

But of course the Wild Bull would not just become a ribeye. Good beef is turned into many cuts, the shoulders would be chuck, then the rib, short loin and Sirloin on the top and the round in the back leg area. Underneath would be the shank and brisket in the front, and then the short plate and flank which would be ground up. Most of these cuts have identifiable steaks and roasts in them. The loin sections, short and sirloin, don't have the annoyance of ribs and make the best steaks, t- bones, sirloins and porterhouse steaks. The ribbed area contains the ribeye from the top and good barbecuing ribs or rib steaks. The shoulders provide good chuck roasts or ground chuck with less fat in it than ordinary ground beef. The leg, sometimes called the rump, provides round steak and cube steaks or can be ground.

Of course, other cuts and steaks and portions could turn the Wild Bull into a sumptuous meal too!

Less than half of a live beef animal can be sold as retail cuts of beef. Hide, internal organs, etc. are a waster of time but other by-products are a little more valuable such as the hide for its leather, tallow, tongue, rennet for cheese making, gelatin for marshmallows, stearin for candy, glycerin for explosives, lanolin for cosmetics, animal fat for soap, camel's hair from cattle ears for artist's brushes, bone charcoal for high grade steel such as ball bearings, glues for plywoods, curled hair for upholstery, etc., etc. Even a cane can be made out of a bull's parts.

One by one, the other cattle were beckoned or downright whipped into entering this little white wooden building and its kill floor.

The Wild Bull was left to last, saving the best for last being Frank's way of thinking. He would have the perfect ribeye for dessert.

And then, Wild Bull really didn't like what he heard at all. The cattle were being shot like common criminals!

And then there were none in the slaughter pen but him.

Frank came out with a bloody leather apron from bib to boot toe.

"Frank", Wild Bull wanted to say, "I think you are letting me down. I was hoping you were the perfect livestocker. I hadn't heard a single complaint from anybody!...Now, I know why!"

"Come on and go with me, little bully, bull, bull," Frank was cooing as he got behind Wild Bull and gave him a little pat on Wild Bull's round steak.

All Wild Bull could do was sneer a little and raise up one corner of his nose in defiance, none of which did any good since the chute into the building was the only way that Wild Bull could go. With every few feet he went, Frank insert a steel gate behind him so he could not retreat backwards. The only way he could go was forward and that seemed to be too easy, like a plan that Wild Bull had not been a willing party to formulating.

Inside the building, Frank placed the last steel gate behind Wild Bull and closed the huge doors hanging on pulleys from the top and latched the doorway with an iron hook.

Wild Bull looked behind himself as well as he could as the doors closed. The blue sky of the spring was disappearing from view. He had never permitted that.

Well, let's see to get back out would require the gate behind him to be dislodged and then he would have to get through those heavy plank doors. No problem with the brute strength force needed, but what about that latch!!!

Soon the coaxing chute pathway ended inside where there was a bloody drain underneath.

In human language he was on the "Kill floor". In Bull language he was at the end of the line.

He could hardly concentrate on what was going on, but what was that he heard? It sounded like a familiar voice out in the public area.

Then Wild Bull returned his attention to the scene in front of him.

"Frank, what are you doing?" Wild Bull asked in a little choked bellow as he observed the salivating butcher cease looking over his ribeye and go over to a butchering table. "I have waited for this moment my entire career," the butcher said to himself with a strange light in his eyes.

Just then the door to the kill floor from the package room opened.

Anna Hackleman entered just as Frank had pulled up the 22 caliber rifle to Wild Bull's head, its barrel shoved between Wild Bull's eyes, his finger itching on the trigger.

One look at Wild Bull from Anna sparked all the recognition needed.

It was the Wild Bull of Blue River! Maybe, Frank didn't recognize him but she did.

Anna knew the Wild Bull well. She had known of him ever since finding Lamb asleep with him down in the crick pasture one night. She had allowed her daughter to lie there so still with the animal who was obviously her pet. She had been so very much a fine young lady then. It must have been in the year before. How long before this had come the petship of the bull and her daughter she did not know but she could guess it had been a long time for the two were as trusting of each other as if they were one. Thereafter, she had always allowed her daughter to have this secret friend. It was a part of the love she had for her daughter that she allowed her daughter to have this secret, this pet bull. Lemuel would never have approved.

Can you imagine that Lemuel thought she did not know her daughter's heart. She did!!!

It was the heart of a child of youth and innocence, a child who had kept a Wild Bull, such a strange creature, as a pet.

Yes, Anna knew all about it. A child cannot keep something dear to her heart from her mother. Anna knew very well about Lamb's Wild Bull, and it had been a secret of their hearts shared but not with Lamb's knowing.

After Lamb's departure, Anna would sometimes go down to the crick where she would take the bull hay. The two became friends drawn together by their missing Lamb.

The Wild Bull was all that was left of the relationship between the mother and daughter. All other ties were gone. Lamb had left long ago. There was not a moment that Anna did not bear in mind the picture of Lamb walking down the farm lane to the road when she left her family home. Anna could never understand why Lamb would not cooperate with her in bringing her back to good reputation by persecuting the offending boy who caused her fall from grace. Surely she would soon come to her senses and return.

But there was a more immediate concern. What was the Wild Bull doing on the kill floor of the Greenfield abattoir?

And one look from Wild Bull to her was all the incentive she needed. That look told Anna all she needed to know. This guy was on the ropes. His count was up. His thread was ready for the scissors.

"Whoa, there Frank," Anna shouted out. "Hey, Hey!!!" the little Deutsch woman insisted.

Frank turned around. He recognized Anna. Then he put the rifle back down beside his leg.

"What you want, Anna?" he asked.

"You hold on, Frank," Anna said. "I'm in a little bit of hurry now to pick up some packages from the freezer," she insisted.

Anna had just come to town to stop at the bakery for some bread, and the abattoir to pick up some meat packages from the last Hackleman butchering.

When the abattoir did custom butchering for patrons, they kept the sides of beef which had been portioned into steaks, and roasts, and ground beef, and other cuts for them in wire baskets inside the packaging room freezer. Two keys were needed. Frank's key was to the outer door. Then the wire cages for individual customers inside were unlocked by patron keys.

"Go, unlock the freezer door for me!" Anna called out insistently. "I mean right now!" the little Deutsch woman demanded.

"Well, okay," Frank said reluctantly since he would have to drop what he was doing.

After Frank left the kill floor and went through the swinging door back into the package room, Anna stayed behind. Then she went over to Wild Bull, "What are you doing here!" she said softly to the quiet bull in a state of shock at the morning's events.

"What do you think!?", Wild Bull seemed to answer. "Not exactly watching daisies grow!"

"Well, Lamb would not like this at all," the little woman said to herself very seriously, her mouth pursed in a look of disapproval.

Quickly, the little woman slipped down behind and unlatched the heavy oak doors and swung them open. Then she swung open the restraining gate behind Wild Bull.

It didn't take Wild Bull long to nod his head "Good-bye" before he had backed out of the kill stall and had hightailed it outside and toward the comforting damp banks of freedom on Brandywine Crick.

Then, just as quickly, Anna slipped back through the chamber and into the packaging room, where Frank had already unlocked the freezer. As Anna went inside to get one of the Hackleman wire baskets of beef, she heard Frank re-entering he kill floor.

And then she heard the shout!

The most civilized of it was the "Damnation!" he expressed. The rest of it related to his carelessness about leaving the gate unlatched when he thought he had it hooked tightly.

Anna went out to the buggy, got in and left, her freezer packages in great disarray beside her on the buggy seat.

As she departed, she noticed Frank heading down the slippery banks of Brandywine after the disappearing Wild Bull of Blue River, and falling on his own round roast from time to time in the mud, only to rise and raise his rifle, blasting in the air only a few shots wildly expended in the general direction of the perfect ribeye.

Why had she burdened this soul, Anna wondered to herself. Perhaps the Wild Bull had been his purchase somehow. No, it would have been impossible. The Wild Bull belonged to providence. He could not have been owned by Frank. Even so, surely, everybody's life is vexed enough without her help!

And then she realized the dark, frustrated but motivating force that had moved her to act,

If she could not save her daughter's life from its off-center sinful course, sheltering a man who had violated her innocence and purity and raped her, perhaps a force of nature could - the Wild Bull of Blue River, who loved her as much as she did. Better to allow the try. It was for sure, with all her bans and imprecations, pleas and unanswered prayers, that Anna could not. Could the Wild Bull have known things that she did not? Did Lamb still maintain contact with her secret pet? Was there some solace possible for her daughter in this beast's company? Was Lamb living a life as vulnerable to death as her pet? Anna could only cringe at the thought of what further pit of sin Lamb might have fallen in.

And then Anna thought to herself: Am I losing my mind to think that a Wild Bull could possibly save my daughter when I cannot?

So many questions were fogging her thinking. One thing was for sure - Anna could not run the race of her daughter's agony with sin begun so unexpectedly in unwed pregnancy.

11

Lamb In Love

"Oh love, what have you done to me?" Lamb cried within. She remembered the warm days in spring when all the world was in extravagant bloom. It had been a time when the earth would not stay still beneath her feet. The minutes pounded each other in her mind and they sent her reeling until she could be with Michael as if a whirlwind were inside demanding release. Her life was shaken to her soul with the love of this neighbor boy, Michael Sipe, and it was a love that demanded she go to him, be with him, and have him by her side. Michael, likewise, could not help wishing rest with Lamb as when bird flies to nest.

The affair had started in the innocence of a youthful dream. They had started out as friends but the feelings grew too strong.

It was Lamb who had gotten herself into this. She would take her Prince of the Land, the Wild Bull, to the County Fair the next August and see him crowned as the finest of the show cattle in the livestock show.

There was only one problem. A girl could not take show cattle into the judging ring. Only a man could do that. The rules of the 1894 County Fair would be the same as those of 1893. She had checked.

And so she had gone to Michael Sipe, the handsome neighbor boy, with a plea and eventually the two had shared Lamb's secret. She had told Michael everything about the Wild Bull, how she had saved him from the cold, how no one in all the world knew about him except for her, and now him, and how she needed Michael's help to prove his worth.

Michael had been filled with the magic of the girl too. He would go see this girl's pet.

Then, swearing him to confidence, she had taken Michael to see Wild Bull out in the woods where twin entwined sycamores marked an entry. Within the roughness of the Blue River was a place apart where no farmer could till and no hunter find easy passage. It was a place fed by springs where wild flowers needed no urging to profuse.

The air was warmly alive and the horizon all around was a band of spring robin egg blue. White gusty clouds overhead were dancing into swoops and swerves filling the sky above with every dance that there could be. There was nothing still in all the airy heavens. It was as if the fresh air close to the ground was playing a game of repel thrusting back up into the heights of the sky the over-exuberant clouds seeking to descend and cover the earth with dazzling white wind.

The woods beneath formed shapes of upward thrusting trees in the whites of the sycamore and browns of the crick willows, while on the upper banks were masses of darkly barked maples and the lighter barked ashes choked by thistling thickets. Green fingers of branches umbrellaed into canopies of leaves darkening the skies so that the crick meadow and woods might be sheltered, warmly wet, and still. The earth offered a refuge here, beneath this overhead fanning of protective leaves, a sanctuary for gentle people and those who might fall into its mood of solitude and softened affections. Near the crick banks were the slashes of muddy slopes, earthy brown barriers, and then the crick itself so steady and bustling at this point in the spring, yet over its raging from the earlier spring drenching rains, raising a merry song of passaging and lapping. It was a place of calm and shelter, safety and hiding, a place where no word could be spoken except softly and without rancor.

Here was the place of the Wild Bull, safeguarded by great and unscalable tree-like walls, entered into by gates of tangling thickets. It was a garden unknown to anyone before its discovery by the little girl in the deep Blue River wilds, hidden from the mere toilers of the land as by angels who had safely guarded it, a point beyond every sea for a gift to a homeless fold, the Deutsch Leute in der neuen Welt, and a place of confidence and promise. In the secret lair of the Wild Bull, Lamb called for her pet to come to her and he did so.

They had cavorted only a little as the Wild Bull had met Michael. He now had two persons he could prance for. Before he had just had Lamb to give nudges to to let her know he still cared.

Then it was time for his bathing. Lamb and then Michael took off their shoes. Michael removed his shirt in the warm late spring day too as they walked down to Dilly Crick through a sandbar narrows. As always, Wild Bull followed. "Wild Bull," Lamb said, "you like this. I know you do."

At the crick, Lamb splashed up some water on her bull's flanks and he started to move and pitch, but as the slightly cooler water filtered through his coat of hair he began to feel better so that he really did kind of like it. Michael had been deputized with some of the lye soap and he took out some soap and rubbed the bull's coat with it until it had foamed and bubbled. The two were becoming wet themselves.

Soon the two kids were laughing and rubbing the pet and soaking him until it was time for a rinse off. Wild Bull turned his head this way and that, trying to take in the impossible look see at what was going on behind him. He was as puzzled about this strange girl and boy and what they were doing to him as he had ever been!

How much fun they seemed to be having, not just with him but with each other! Wild Bull would hold steady and try to listen carefully to their words, these unaccountable human sounds, that Michael kept saying to her. "Lamb, I will help you with this bull whenever you wish me to. All you will have to do is call, and I will say, 'I am here.'"

"Isn't he beautiful, Michael," Lamb said. "Do you like my pet?"

"He is not nearly so beautiful as you, Lamb," the boy wished to say but in the confusion of his thoughts, he could not.

Lamb asked Michael, "Will you help me to present him in the ring at the county fair as the greatest animal in the world with the very best possible manners?" The Wild Bull himself hung on these words spoken so urgently and with his beloved mistress looking so beseechingly into this attractive young man's blue eyes.

Whatever she was saying, she seemed happy with the response, Wild Bull decided, so he let this strange ritual go on! He already felt like the King of the World simply because his Lamb, and now this young man that she had chosen to come to their secret lair, was with him.

When Wild Bull was as clean as any animal ever was or could be, Lamb walked out of the stream bed. She went over to the sycamore and found her shoes and put them back on. Wild Bull shook and wiggled to rid himself of his excess water from his scrubbing. Michael put back on his shirt and slipped on his shoes. Yes, they would see each other often.

As the springtime proceeded, did Michael see that her face showed every infatuation? Lamb sometimes wondered. Being 16 and in love was not an easy thing to hide. Why did she sense in Michael's eyes the same look, the demands and deepest urges causing him to fumble and hem haw at times. They must touch. They must trust each other. Otherwise they would be walking in a black night.

The spring had begun so innocently with the two stealing away at every time they could to the secret lair of the Wild Bull in the wilds of the Blue River Valley. The young and growing up need to have their days so full of activity. There must not be a moment of time wasted! The two would not leave even a click of time unused. They would tend to their charge, the Wild Bull, now a powerfully portioned bull, and obviously a worthy competitor for any prize at the fair. The bull thrived on the attention of the two and pranced and performed for them.

But more than that. When the two, Lamb and Michael, would enter the secret place unknown to the world, it was as if their thoughts were abandoned and dreams of each other took their places. The walk through the woods to the lair did not just separate them from their lives as Deutsche Kinder but with every step their fears were scaled away, the defenses to each other's souls flew, and passion filled their eyes as they looked to each other. At first Lamb

was afraid, but the fear was cast away because love, a stronger emotion, convinced her that she must allow her life to flow as does
every river. There is no crick that can stop its ebb and no dam that
can withstand a flood.

The warmth of these days caused the scene to blur into its pri-
mal colors. Its immoderation was as a painter's with brush daubed
in blue for a sky so shining and new, a dazzling zinc white for a
horizon with no more than hints of anything specific, tones of
greens, oranges and browns for the earth, and a mimicking trans-
parency for the waters. Such colors in broad swaths were all that it
was necessary to see. The land did not require closer inspection on
these days of the two in the lair of the Wild Bull. All was favorable.
Everything fun. Life was looked at as from a magnifying glass held
at a distance and thus without focus as to a reality which might
inject too stark a response to what they were doing. The warmth
was not just in the scene either. It was also in the heart of the boy
and girl who needed to distinguish nothing except the presence of
the other and the company of the Wild Bull of Blue River.

The Wild Bull would await them in their coming and greet
each with the rub of a very large and unusual pet. And the two, the
boy and girl, would go through their training, with Michael taking
the bull into a halter, and walking him, giving him the instructions
in a talk which the Wild Bull seemed to come to understand. Yes,
Wild Bull would mind this boy who was in the company of this girl.
Lamb acted as though she wanted him to and if his beloved Lamb
wished him to perform he would take any role under the stars!

But this distraction did not prevail. It would be no use pre-
tending. The boy and the girl were in love. Michael found the
strength to tell Lamb that they must let their love show. He convinced her that he could not hold out any longer, that they had no
reason to fear. Lamb knew no restraint either. They gave themselves
over to this love without a backward glance until its fire flooded
their souls. They held back nothing and neither held back any
secret. They could be imagined as one, whether it was right or
wrong did not matter. Their love went beyond the question of what
was right and what was wrong. Could it be expected that a flower

should not blossom? Such a thing is impossible. Lamb and Michael allowed their love to blossom into full bloom. They crossed every threshold with each other as if in a dream, promising all the while that there would never be an end to their sharing in this lifetime. Lamb felt so secure with Michael! What they were doing had to be right! To Michael, Lamb made every doubt about his life clear. She had saved him from his solitude.

The Wild Bull's care became every occasion they would need to be with each other. One day, Lamb decided to make Wild Bull's head look even better by clipping the hair coat up to a point about 3 inches back of the ears. She had tried it before and Wild Bull looked so handsome!

Would Michael allow her to clip his long blond hair that fell down to his shoulders? Once while lying so still on the meadow embankment, Lamb had snuck up behind him to clip its strands. She would have done it in a flick if he had not turned and caught her in the act of sneaking up on him. Did he not know the story of Samson!

Afterwards they wrestled until she became convinced he would not allow it. But their closeness was as it always was, a time when they knew the joy of each other. Michael and she were one in spirit, both foolish and crazy about each other. He was always careful not to hurt her and keep her from harm's way.

One of these delicious days, Michael's shirt slipped off the crick rock where he had cast it and was floating downstream. The object was a fascination to the Wild Bull and he went after it, catching it on his horn and returning it to Michael on the embankment with Lamb. With laughter, Michael and Lamb accepted back this retrieval. Even miraculous things seemed to be happening in these bounteous and blooming woods, nurtured by the laughing waters of their crick hideaway.

Michael promised Wild Bull an ear of corn if he could do the same trick the next day. All seemed wonder. All of nature was joining them in their love - a never-ending song.

The next day, Michael placed his shirt upon the same rock where it would again fall into the crick and, while he and Lamb watched, the Wild Bull again performed the same retrieval from its watery downstream journey, and received the corn Michael had promised as a reward.

After succeeding days the two would laughingly come to call the game, "Gore and fetch." Here on the crick meadow, there was held up no heavy hand of the world. Here no unkind word could be spoken or evil intention intrude. Not even a thought about the future was necessary because the warm days so filled their lives that there was no room for doubting that the happy music of time was on their side and its day would never end. Wild Bull came to enjoy "Gore and fetch," as much as he enjoyed everything else about being with Michael and Lamb.

Here where they loved each other in the presence of the Wild Bull, there could be nothing wrong in life, no hell, except where the three were parted or they had lost the feelings that life was as tender as the meadow grass.

These days, there never was a day when the two did not slip away to their secret place on the Blue River where the Wild Bull would greet them and they would not encounter their passion. They gave up their fight against their feelings which they could fight no longer. Their meetings were as necessary as the risings of the sun in the sky and as inevitable as the sun in its setting. Though their feet might seem to be merely walking, their souls were soaring as they left the beaten farm paths and meadow grasses to reach their place of loving. They seemed closer every day to reaching the secret of life. It must be true. Love lasts forever!

But now came August. They would test out their Prince, the Wild Bull, against all other creatures of the universe.

Michael had not come yet but was due to arrive any minute. Lamb could not help but sing as she arose to the morning's dawn. The winds accompanied as with trumpeting brassy melodies. The show would be in six hours and there was much to be done, even more than had already been done. Lamb was exhausted now emotionally. How would she feel later? Who says when you are 16 you have boundless energy?

A robin was already tchk-tchk-tchking through yellow beak, strutting on her windowsill, its tail at a perky angle, as Lamb had slipped out of her bed at dawn. Soon Lamb sneaked into the Hoosier crick woods to call Wild Bull. "Now let's get you bathed and shaved and groomed," Lamb said. "Michael will soon be here," she whispered.

What kind of nonsense is this? Wild Bull wondered. After his bath, Lamb took out from her pocket a little tin of polish and had him stand still as she rubbed the polish into the horns to make them glisten and shine. "You are going to have the best looking horns of, well, ever!" she told her beloved pet, insisting that he stand still and stop trying to nudge and rub. He did insist on doing just a little bit of rubbing back so that when she got her hands on his horns, he got his nose into her tummy until she had to giggle and he to snort.

After working on Wild Bull's head, Lamb had him stand very still out there where the sun was beginning its journey into the sky while she took out the clippers and began to clip his tail from the tailhead to the bottom of the twist. Then she just touched up his tailhead a bit too.

Wild Bull went along with it, but he would have liked to swat her a little with his tail just to see if this was some lashing game of some kind. What could all this be leading up to, Wild Bull wondered? This kid is up to something. "Wild Bull." Lamb told him, sensing a little uneasiness, "now don't you worry about a thing. Your tail is going to look as handsome as the rest of you!" And then when she was through clipping, she brushed and fluffed out his tail switch until it was as fluffy as a dandelion to seed.

By this time, Wild Bull's coat was pretty well dried out so that Lamb could give it a good brushing too. Soon Michael was there and he brought with him some coat-dressing to apply. The judges would be impressed! He would just put a hint of it on. It would take away points if he put even so much as to cause two hairs to stick together. Wild Bull wiggled with every rub, but held steady wondering if Michael really knew what he was doing. He had never had that stuff on before! Maybe it would keep the horn flies off.

Then Lamb and Michael both combed his coat to smooth it out. Wild Bull's hair wasn't long enough to curl or cull as some beef cattle's coats are. He was lucky really, not to have a really heavy coat. It turns a cow nervous and anxious in the heat of summer. Wild Bull wasn't bald by any means. He just had a nice smoothable coat. The judges wouldn't be impressed by a really curly animal anyway. Usually, a thick, heavy coat is only left on to camouflage weakness in conformation anyway. Wild Bull didn't have to worry about weakness or poor features.

After they combed him over, they put their brushes away.

Finally, before leaving to the road, Lamb took out a halter and came to Wild Bull and told him, "I don't want you messing your beautiful self up now!" She looked Wild Bull straight in the eye. He could never outstare her although they sometimes played that game too. This time when he looked at her back, he got the message, "Hey, she means business about something."

As he held his head steady, he felt the halter being placed over his head. "Lamb," he wanted to say and would have if he could have talked, "I don't like this part! I know what you are dooooo-ing!" But, so what, if he was willing to put up with the rest, maybe he could hold off stomping about back in the woods, resting at his favorite bank or rubbing on his favorite tree, just a while. Wasn't it his Lamb who was in charge of him and doing this?

Lamb made sure the nose strap of the halter was adjusted and exactly midway between Wild Bull's eyes and nose. Yes, that was just right.

Then she pulled the halter over-strap behind his ears and did some more adjusting until everything was just right. Then she tied the halter behind the sycamore until Michael was ready with the team and trailer they would drive to the fair. Soon, Wild Bull and Lamb heard Michael shout, "Let's go to the Fair!"

12

Wild Bull To The County Fair

And now it was time for Lamb and Michael to take the Wild Bull to the Hancock County Fair.

The National Road was filled with fairgoers as the three approached Greenfield. What a busy place it was. Michael pointed out to Lamb the new paper mill being built on the corner of the National Road and Morristown Pike as they passed by. "They are opening even now and taking on new employees," he had heard.

The fair was further around the perimeter of the city to the north. From that short distance away, there ahead were the gas balloons rising to the sky! Both Michael and Lamb had heard of the gas balloon rides that would take fairgoers to the skies. The fair had to be close now!

Watch out! As the two closed in on the Morristown Pike, riders were appearing, contestants in the road races underway. Several horses were speeding down the Morristown Pike hell bent for leather. Here was a sorrel taking a lead by a head.

It would be better, the two thought, to unload the Wild Bull at the neck of the meadow of the Brandywine Crick north of the National Road and walk him down its meandering to the fair not so far from the Brandywine ford just beyond and up the rise from the abattoir.

The walk was so very pleasant with Michael leading and Lamb aside her Wild Bull there on the banks where the merry waters of the crick sang as they rippled. Only once did they stop in their march to the fairgrounds and that was to give the Wild Bull a drink at the ford itself while they sat on the warm sod of the banks, hands held with hopes dancing.

Not much later the two crossed the crick and entered the fairgrounds. They would need to pass by the Floral Pavilion and the sideshow tents on their way to the stock sheds and the show ring tent.

The Fair would be the most fun of any place in the world just then.

Here a tent with huge sign fronting announcing the presence of "Little Egypt" in these very parts. Noised about everywhere among the gentlemen and boys, this dancer was said to know the seductive Arabic dances of the steamy Nile. Upon a stage to its side performed a four- piece band with two banjo players, a drummer, and a man in striped shirt with harmonica alternately lilting out musical notes and singing their lyrics. American flags were everywhere, over every sign, and waving at angles from all of the fair's tents, rides and buildings. At the next tent were four huge signs beside an entry to a sideshow depicting a man living with a shaft through his head, an alligator boy, a fat lady weighing over 500 pounds, guaranteed, and a man who could eat fire.

Crowds were everywhere around the fair, especially around the tents. Many were standing in a knot in front of the loudly strutting banjo band. The women were with their straw hatted men, except that the women were wearing the whitest dresses while the men were in the darkest suits so that the contrast provided a study in light and dark. Most of the buggies and horses were parked near the entrance but occasionally there was a temporary call to "Make way" between the tents as some personage of importance would drive his carriage to one spot or another. Strings of pennants connected the tents. Some talk was of the night's pie eating contest and other was of the sack races scheduled for the next day.

To the side of the main road were the gas balloon rides and a merry-go-round with steam engine cranking for a spin and loud music blaring with a heavy beat. Barkers' calls filled whatever tiny crack of silence might otherwise have dared to slink in.

Lamb and Michael passed by all of this to lead Wild Bull to the show tent where the judging of livestock would soon occur. After they arrived, they waited impatiently along with some others with their contesting cattle. The show clerk now came out to where the contestants were gathered, Michael and Lamb and Wild Bull with the rest, and checked each's age and weight classification and listed them by their owners as he reached them. Each was also given a number in huge black script to pin to the back of their shirts.

Michael had the huge black number three in Arabic script to pin on his back.

Wild Bull was number 3.

Lamb winked to Michael as he went inside the show tent with Wild Bull.

She shouted out, "Good luck!" as she saw him disappear into the side of the tent opened by huge tent flaps. She couldn't wait to enter through the side flap and soon she found a seat in the bleacher stands overlooking the ring.

Michael searched the stands after settling down his place in the line. Yes, there was Lamb. My, he thought to himself, how beautiful was this impossible neighbor girl who he would do anything for. She was more beautiful than any woman he had ever seen.

But his mind must not wander. Michael soon concentrated and became oblivious to everything except taking the ringmaster's final instructions. Yes, there were the three judges who were introduced to the crowd by their last names of Douthett, Elsbury and Weber. Michael looked over to them quizzically, wondering if they could come to appreciate and admire Wild Bull as much as he and Lamb did.

A younger boy was beside him with his steer. He looked over at Michael and half whispered, "They look as tough as nails! They do!" He too had noticed the judges approaching the scene.

And the judges were noticing back.

The little group of show folk brought their charges out into the ring.

Michael held the lead strap in his right hand while parading out the Wild Bull, leading him from the left side and holding the lead strap in his right hand as closely from 1 to 2 feet from the head as possible and at the height of the top of his head. The effect was that of discipline, steadiness, control, and would highlight an animal's responsive obedience. The extra length of lead strap Michael carried in the form of several large loops in his same hand. All of this had been carefully rehearsed.

The judges watched as the animals followed each other out into the center of the ring. One of the animals jostled a bit and even started at another animal. That would lose points. In such an exhibition, a showman avoids having his animal come in contact with a competitor or encroaching upon space rightfully in possession of another show animal.

The show was underway! The competing men and boys were as much of the show as their animals, each trying to appear entirely emotionless so as to avoid detracting from their animal.

When Michael was walking Wild Bull about the ring, he could glance at the other stock. Some had such obvious defects. How he would have loved to call out to the judge, "Look at that one's very small frame. Humpffff. And that one should be docked for weight, don't you think? It couldn't weigh 800 pounds. And that one's back looks like a saggy mattress." But of course he could not. A show person can never refer to a competing animal. It is just not allowed, Nor could Michael point out all of Wild Bull's innumerable and totally obvious strengths.

All Michael could do was to keep positioning Wild Bull so that it would be convenient for the judge to see every single one of Wild Bull's perfect features well and frequently. And that is exactly what he did.

As the judges approached Wild Bull, Michael placed him in a proper position for the benefit of the judge's inspection.

When the time came for positioning from a stand, Wild Bull remained steady and Michael stood facing him holding the lead strap in his left hand. So what was so hard about that for Wild Bull? He kind of liked looking on Michael face to face. And Wild Bull showed his content with the arrangement by standing with his back level, head up and alert, and with a "foot under each corner." Why shouldn't he be standing proud. Wasn't it Michael with him?

One of the judges asked whether Michael had purchased him or had him bred. Michael answered promptly with the fact that his was a winter birth on the farm.

Then the judges walked away to observe all of the entries, moving around to inspect every vantage. To show Wild Bull required Michael to keep on his toes, to know constantly the whereabouts of each of the three judges so that Wild Bull would be in the best spot if the judge should even happen to glance in his direction as each worked the ring.

All of this was quite unnecessary as far as Wild Bull was concerned. He got the drift of what was happening the moment he saw all these other cattle around. He could show himself quite well, never you mind! These other cattle were just clowns, grandstanders. He eyed the competition and knew he had it made from the start.

He and Michael were an unbeatable team. The world just might as well know it. He could tell. Look at the pride Lamb and Michael shower on me, he thought to himself. Don't forget Lamb is impressive too. But she is not in the ring so I will have to be impressive for both of us. Michael bore a silent, confident attitude about his charge through it all.

While two of the judges appeared to be in rather good humors one assumed the air of a Scottish Yard detective in ferreting out weakness. He had approached two others, and now came to Wild Bull.

He said evenly to Michael, "Please take this animal out of line."

Michael was confused. What did this mean? Had Wild Bull flunked? But he must do as bid even if it meant ruin. Michael followed the etiquette he recalled when given this cue by a judge. He was to back Wild Bull out of line, not lead him out in the clockwise movement that is a point of scoring in showing cattle. Michael did so, but would Wild Bull follow this unusual and demanding maneuver?

Would Michael for the first time be required to use his show stick to gain Wild Bull's cooperation?

Michael moved back himself in the start of the complex maneuver. All of the other judges paused. None had requested this maneuver of any of the others. All contestants dread its command. Even the stands quieted as they saw this handsome young man with the long shoulder length blond hair turn his show stock, in the midst of his competitors who themselves had turned to see what would come of this. All hushed to see the outcome.

Michael took his first step backward maintaining a confident composure as required of show persons, but feeling queasy and unsure down deep. "Wild Bull, please back out of line with me," he said without vocalizing. "Follow me in rear march."

While the judge waited, hand cupped in chin, Michael took another step backward. The judge had already made up his mind. If his show animal could do this, the judge would award this animal the grand championship as being the finest of the show cattle.

"Please, Wild Bull," Michael prayed again.

And backward Wild Bull stepped. If Michael wanted to play a backing game, so did he. And back he stepped again and again until Michael himself stopped!

And still the judge did not move, but remained looking at the animal quizzically.

What more could he want from us? Michael thought to himself.

"Oh no," he said to himself and looked at his own feet. They were not squared, one foot was out ahead of the other. And then, in horror, he looked at Wild Bull's feet too and so were Wild Bull's. Quickly Michael adjusted his feet so that both were squared. Wild Bull ever observant and willing to follow Michael in every maneuver to his own death, adjusted his fore and hind feet into their correct squared position too.

The cattle tent saw this showmanship with awe. A mere animal here there was before them, but one totally committed to its showman's command. Whether wrong or right, the animal would follow the showman's bidding. The trust and love that this indicated! The trust and love this indicated!

And the lead judge himself, an old man of his sixties, the most rigorous of them all, and fastidious, and demanding, removed the cup of his palm from his chin, and to the amazement of the entire class of spectators, looked at Michael and smiled, and before you know it he did something else...He clapped his hands in appreciation.

And when the others who had witnessed the event saw the maneuver, the response and the witness of the judge himself, they too began to clap and the applause was shared with smiles of appreciation as Wild Bull, as if to acknowledge, shook his head with eyes raised in a nod, only once, and then resumed his show position and returned to the line.

Not much later, the judges handed the clerk the order of their judging.

The clerk arose to announce the decision and the small crowd of onlookers was brought to attention.

"The winner and grand champion Hancock County Beef is," and he coughed just a bit, "Number Three, shown by Michael Sipe."

Michael had to smile so broadly and proudly. The only person who was there to share this success was Lamb and looking about he found her jumping up and down in the stands. Her exuberance was as the sparkling of a rocket.

He was standing up with his hands waving in the air, and his shouts of "Yahooooooooo" were equally obvious to the rest of the crowd and to the world of its reverberating air.

Michael joined his happy look only for an instant before becoming the show person again, being a modest winner at least while in public. He accepted graciously the congratulations of the winner of the runner-up honor as etiquette required.

Michael and Lamb had won it all with Wild Bull. They could see Jerusalem come down. For himself, Wild Bull stayed in the ring until the class was fully placed and records completed before he left first of the class. This too is etiquette. Retirement from the ring takes place in the order of the placing of the class.

And Wild Bull had Michael and Lamb with him. Wild Bull was proud too. He had been proven to be the finest Bull in all the world once and for all. No doubt about it. No competition. The world was afire with flushness.

Then Michael returned to the meadow to release the Wild Bull to his lair. Lamb and Michael would play one last game of "Gore and fetch" this day as they had been playing it with the Wild Bull in many variations. This time Michael wrapped the championship cup from the fair in his shirt and threw it to the waves where Wild Bull retrieved it to them on the banks as would a little happy puppy.

Now, before their parting on this day of proof that love prevails, the two would again confess to each their love as always. Should Lamb tell Michael this day that she had learned she was pregnant? No, better to tell her mother first, the person who would know best what to do.

Lamb had given Michael no clue that he had caused her to become pregnant. The fact was a surprise to her, something she had never stopped to think about happening. Being pregnant? It was beyond contemplating within the muddle of her mind in the happy glows of life with Michael. She would get the advice of her mother first before telling Michael that he was soon to become a father!

On this day of happiness, nothing could go wrong. Now would be the time to reveal her pregnant condition to Anna, her own life-giver.

Lamb felt there could be nothing wrong with the world. She must tell her mother this very day, while everything was right with the world, that she was pregnant. Flush from the victorious showing of her pet bull, trouble had to be far away. She kissed Michael good-bye with every ounce of her love and hope for the future.

The steps to her mother's chair in the parlor were not fearful. She would quickly reveal to her mother that she was pregnant, something would be worked out. Perhaps her mother would share the joy in the discovery that she herself had felt, and that would be that.

She could pray for this result.

Lamb found her mother seated in the Hackleman home's parlor. This room always seemed so foreboding with its wallpaper of monotonously dark green and rich patterning, shapes as stylized tulips dignified into repetitious lines. Lamb found Anna sitting there on a parlor chair next to the end table with its waxed bouquet giving off no scent. The room was so dark this day. Even where the upholstery of the sofa was flowery patterned, the impression was that whatever flowers would have been bright and fresh in the natural outdoors were dark and trepidatious inside. Lamb went to stand by a pot of woods ferns incongruously removed from their natural setting and permitted only the light filtered through windows covered by heavy damask curtains suspended upon a bronze rod. Anna had looked up to see her daughter before her.

"Mother, I am pregnant," Lamb told Anna. Anna's face had dropped and its expression was a look Lamb had never seen before. It was not merely disappointment, nor anger, nor frustration, but the fullness of them all out of control. Anna lost all composure. She had been told something too shocking for her emotional handling.

Here this selfsame day of joy had become the day when Anna told Lamb she must betray the boy who had gotten her in trouble and see him prosecuted and jailed for rape or else leave the home. Anna would personally see him driven into hell and kill him herself if she had to.

And on the selfsame day in which Wild Bull had proved that love triumphs, Lamb herself would be placed to the same test. Could she be the cause of Michael's downfall, he who had given her the spring and summer while lying by her side?

There was only the one course of action for her to take. And as Lamb left her girlhood home she had in her recollection the new Greenfield paper mill recently built and hiring. Should she go to see Michael? No, it might lead to his indictment or Michael confronted with her father or mother with rifle or some other danger. Her heart was in flames.

How she wished she could have said to Anna, "But I love the boy more than I love my own life. He is kind and good and when I am with him I feel sheltered from the world and safe from any harm. And mother, he loves me more than you can ever know." No such words could have been spoken to Anna after hers of condemnation. Lamb's little Deutsch mother had already made up her mind about the boy's ill worth, whoever he might be. It did not matter who he might be. He must be punished horribly. She would kill him herself if she could, this one who had brought stain on her spotless Lamb.

Lamb half remembered her final words to her mother, "Mother, I will never see the boy hurt for what he and I have done!" She would accept that her life must be one lived in contempt in a world that would hate her for loving too strongly and cast her aside into a life of disgrace. She would survive for the sake of her baby growing within her. She must leave her home to protect Michael. She would honor her parents by causing their family name to bear no taint of having an immoral daughter with child out of wedlock.

Only one thing did she take with her - a secret known and trusted in her heart: that the love which she had known from man and family would somehow never die. It would be the manna for her journey through the wilderness days to come.

Greenfield would be ahead - up the road a few miles. A girl might be able to find work there.

13

A Gypsy Encounter

It was August, 1894, and the days burned.

This day as before and always Michael Sipe's eyes were mischievously and fallaciously seeing Lamb Hackleman before him. She seemed always there in the vicinity of his heart, just out of reach, but such a beckoning thought nevertheless! Michael reached for the saddle horn of his horse, Red, and swung himself up onto the saddle. He would take a ride into Greenfield. He needed to get away from the farm for a few minutes. Some purpose was in his mind that needed to be played out. Perhaps a ride would help get Lamb off his mind. Impossible! Possible? Lamb Hackleman! She was as a candle shining in a window of a warm home to a winter traveler needing shelter. Could he get her off his mind, ever? With thought of Lamb, Michael clucked in Red's ear and heeled his flank. Surely there must be some more immediate errand buzzing in the back of his mind that he would recall once he was on his way.

In Oklahoma this same August day the air was hot and the grass browning and dry. Oh well, the day's activities still had to be done! At the Ferree home, Lamb had long been at work at the paper mill, since dawn, but to the Ferrees, with whom she lived, there were groceries to be seen to. Adam Ferree, the man of the house, had to leave this chore to his wife. His shattered feet, ruined in a factory accident at the Conklin Iron Works, did not permit him to hobble very far.

Mrs. Ferree, Pleasant's baby-sitter, would simply take her walk out into the country to buy the brown eggs the next mile down from the workers' camp along the National Road. On her arm was her egg basket and in front of her was a little cart on wooden wheels made by her husband out of a grocery box. She was going to take the baby with her. Pleasant, Lamb's little child, approaching two, would enjoy the summer day. Mrs. Ferree liked taking Pleasant with her. He was coming along so nicely now, just able to walk, a little early. He was exceptional. Many children do not learn to walk with such a stride as did Pleasant until they are further into life.

Mrs. Ferree found the farmhouse on the National Road where she had often bought the brown eggs she and her husband liked. Leaving Pleasant in his cart by the front door, Mrs. Ferree, her egg basket on her arm, went with the farmwife to the barn behind the house where the chickens laid their eggs in the straw. There was always a little bit of hunt and seek in the egg purchasing venture. That made it fun even for a grown woman. Here's one, Mrs. Ferree, over by the axe near the log at the wood pile even before getting to the barn! Inside the barn, there are several by the ladder stairs and scattered on the straw of the wagon floor and in the stalls' hay racks.

But what is this! As the two, the buyer and seller, were at their egg hunt, a squawk was heard outside in the barnlot. Running out to see what was happening, the farmwife saw a dark-skinned boy running out of the barnlot with a laying chicken held tightly by the legs. His ballooning trousers and bright red shirt gave him away as a Gypsy boy.

Shouting did no good to stop him. Her cries of "Stop, thief!" did not even cause the boy to glance around. He was out of there! He must have been in his early teenage years.

When Mrs. Ferree came sauntering out of the barn a little later, her egg basket almost filled, she saw the boy make a turn around the side of the house, stop briefly at the little cart in which Pleasant was sleeping and take off again.

What could he have been doing at Pleasant's cart, Mrs. Ferree wondered, and then fear clutched her. She dropped her egg basket to the ground. The eggs, many now cracked, were the farthest things on her mind.

It took Mrs. Ferree about the time lightning takes to strike to reach the cart and looking inside she found that Pleasant was gone. Up ahead far down the National Road to the East she saw the boy with both arms loaded, one with the squawking chicken and the other with the little boy bouncing along on his shoulder.

For the longest time there seemed nothing to do. Neither Mrs. Ferree nor the farmwife was herself youthful or runner.

The two women realized they must get help. The farmwife ran toward the back acreage to get her husband who was working there. Mrs. Ferree could do no more than stand at the roadway, shocked, frantic, wide-eyed and crazed, hoping for help to arrive.

The farm lady's run ended with a greeting to her husband out in the field. She shouted to him to come quickly for a child had been kidnapped by the Gypsies. The man was sweating profusely. His felt hat was blotched with sweat as was the whole front beneath his armpits of the white shirt, long- sleeved, he was wearing. He jumped off his wheeled cultivator and setting a foot on the metal spoke of one of its iron wheels, removed his hat and scratched his head. Even after hearing the news he continued scratching his head. Ahead of him were his team of mules, ears pointy and nervous about the delay. Only when they were moving did the fly chaser strips of leather netted on their backs flip over and offer these animals relief from the late summer horse flies. Finally, despite his wife's hysteria, the old man told her matter of factly, "Won't do no good chasin' after Gypsies," he told her. "You know that as well as I do."

"Well, we got to try, Samuel," the egg-lady insisted. "We can't leave some child to a Gypsy life!"

"Won't help," the old man insisted. "They hide 'em and then they run off so's no one can find them." But the old man sadly acknowledged that he must go to see about this need and leave the field so in need of his cultivating. Even so, he knew the warnings of common knowledge in the neighborhood. Any who crossed the Gypsies or angered them might find his barn unaccountably burned down. Knowing this dampened the man's enthusiasm for he was elderly now and needed peace not mischief pulled on him.

Mrs. Ferree had become hysterical by the time the old man driving his team of mules and the egg- lady returned, except that with mounting hope she saw a man riding his horse toward town who would soon pass her way. Would he respond to her call for help? It was Michael Sipe.

As soon as he was within call, Ms. Ferree began her cries, "Help! Help!" she was screaming. "A baby has been kidnapped! The Gypsies got a baby!"

Michael Sipe brought his horse to a gallop to come quickly, then shouted for his horse, Red, to "Whoa."

In strained voice, barely making sense, Mrs. Ferree explained the situation, how the baby had been kidnapped by the Gypsy boy.

"Whose baby is it? Yours?" Michael enquired.

"No, but I watch him during the day. The mother is a mill girl. I saw a Gypsy boy grab the child and take off," she explained again.

You must help this woman, Michael heard a voice within himself demand. It was as a ghost, an apparition, tugging and demanding from within his heart.

Michael drew his horse to her side. "You must jump on ma'am." If he were to help her he must have her with him to help identify the child should he come across it. In the back of his mind was the question whether he should call for the posse. There is strength in numbers. Confronting a band of Gypsies by himself could be dangerous or deadly. Yet time raised its hand. By the time it would take to gather his friends in the horse thief protection company, the Gypsies might move on if they were on the lam or perhaps hide the child outside their encampment. He would risk himself and summon the magic of surprise. It might prove the only chance to recover the child. They would not expect a single horseman to come after a child. Yes, he must see to this business by himself or else this child might be lost to this woman and the child's mother back in Oklahoma forever. There seemed no time to lose.

The lady uncomfortably swung herself on the horse seating herself behind Michael on his mount and hugged him with all her bulk in an awkward effort to find the balance to stay on. How lucky she was, she thought, to find this young man so eager to help. She didn't even mind holding on to him so tightly since he was so good looking. Now her luck must hold! Michael leaned forward and heeled at Red's flank to speed him into a gallop. There must be no time wasted.

Seeing the help arrived and the woman and Michael off on their quest, the old man said to his farmwife, "She has far better help than I can offer." He would go back to his cultivating. No point in arousing such a dangerous tribe as these Gypsies must be against him if they would stoop to kidnapping.

As they drove the road, Michael turned his head to Mrs. Ferree to ask if she knew of the whereabouts of the Gypsies.

The woman shouted into his ear that "No" but she had seen the boy run off to the east.

After passing several farm homes on the way, Michael interrogated a child in front of one of them who claimed to have seen some Gypsy wagons pulling off the Range Line road, some with their one or two head of cattle tethered on the wagon's rear. That road slash was only half a mile ahead.

At the intelligence, Michael returned his horse to a gallop with portly Mrs. Ferree precariously holding on behind, her eyes closed and buttocks pounding on the horse's back like repetitive billowing whitecaps crashing on the shore. Michael was after the kidnapping vagabond as a hound pursuing coon.

The Gypsies were never welcome in their passage through the county, not because they were poor, or strange looking, or because they could hardly be understood in their speech, but because neighbors always seemed to come up missing things after they left. But of course the roads were open to all travelers, Gypsies as well as others.

Up ahead, the Gypsy wagons could be observed. Several vardos, as the Gypsy wagons were called, were encamped in the schoolyard of a little one- room school, called Simmon's Corner, or School No.2 of Jackson Township, just north of the starkly white clapboarded Brown's Chapel Church. Gypsies often used such places as this unused school, whose term would not come to session until later in the year, for temporary occupation. Here ahead were "the secret people" who referred to themselves as Romani but which those in the Deutsch neighborhoods called Gypsies. They could read the future in the outstretched palm of a person and gage the meanings of the stars. They mysteriously would appear where other Gypsies had previously encamped. It was said there were strange signs, pookerin' koshes, which only the Romani knew of, hidden along the National Road which would direct them to their safe overnight places such as this one. These strange road markings could never be found by any to obliterate.

Fleecy clouds in the sky flew over the encampment and the sun shining through them as it went sent similarly cloud-shaped shadows racing over the hot landscape.

Michael rode toward their wagons. To the side were the horses drawn off. The wagons were settled for the day with their shafts dropped to the front like open forks with little steps to the half-doorways between. Many were straight-sided but a few had skylights. Each had a stack emerging from the curved roof, the vent for a wood-burning stove within. Paintwork was on the sides of them, arrayed in the brightest colors of the earth, reds, blues, greens and yellows and embellished with fine carving. A single one was an open-ender with a canvas tilt.

Michael knew of this mysterious people by reputation. Their customs were of common knowledge. Michael knew he could expect to find the baby only, if at all, in the custody of one of the women of the Gypsies and in one of their wagons. It would not be that a man of the Romani would hand over the child, for to the Gypsies this was a voodoo and curse and frightful and horrible things were thought to happen to any Gypsy man who held a child.

The Gypsies did not like visitors coming within the circle of their wagons, especially in the daunting and challenging way in which Michael acted in this day with the strange-acting and nearly hysteric woman, Mrs. Ferree, now crying out and holding her behind from the horse riding.

"Gorgio!" a child shouted as Michael dismounted. This was a general name in their language for any non-Gypsy.

"Sar shan," a man said at a campfire as Michael approached. It was the greeting of the travelers. The man was strange to behold, carrying a tambourine, wild looking and yet with a dark expressionless face and jet black hair. He was lean and dressed in dark clothing, a jacket and pants that hung down over his gaunt lower frame except at the knee where the trousers were ripped and his knee emerged. But around his neck was a brilliant dash of color, a yellow scarf as bright as a field canary. Michael did not return a friendly greeting. "Where is the child recently kidnapped?" he asked the man.

Women and children came about. The man raised his shoulders in a shrug. Then shaking his head, the man turned to walk away. He began to call some of the other men to come from their wagons. Some did, with long knives by their sides.

But there would be no intimidating Michael or stopping him from his mission. Michael sneered at the men as he walked over to the first wagon. Climbing its short steps to the door, he looked inside and then climbed back down. At the second wagon, there was a big woman wearing a huge handkerchief over her white hair which billowed out from beneath, her face lined and wrinkled, her mouth clamped tightly around a clay pipe. She held in her hand an ax head on a splintered ax handle. Michael looked inside this wagon. No child. He left as the woman cursed him loudly. Had she wielded the ax and killed him and then Mrs. Ferree, no one outside the encampment would have ever known. Yet, some force restrained her hand from finishing the task.

Another man and woman came up to him, the man gripping a long knife he had drawn from its sheath. They said nothing but it was clear they would accompany Michael on any further searching.

The Gypsy people had all now come to watch, the men dressed plainly but the women in shawls and sashes and brightly colored garments.

The earlier searching had had the advantage of surprise, but that element was now gone as the word of this intruder had spread through the camp. Now as all of the group seemed to converge upon Michael, he confronted them. "We demand the return of a kidnapped child," Michael said.

One of the Gypsy men, the leader it must have been, responded with a waving knife and a demand that Michael and this woman leave. "Not without the baby," Michael said. "Either you turn him over or I call the neighbor men of the posse and they have a little habit of torching wagons of kidnappers and stringing up any's not cooperative."

As the confrontation was at an impasse, Mrs. Ferree took up with a yelp and tugged at Michael's shirt. "There is the boy that run off with him," Mrs. Ferree shouted as she saw a boy wearing a bright red shirt disappear into one of the wagons.

Michael went over to his mount, eyeing the man with the knife in a dare to try it, and drew from his saddle the rifle he kept at its side.

"I suggest you all clear out," he said as he walked over to the wagon where the boy had disappeared. As Michael drew to the door, the red- shirted boy jumped out and ran. Inside Michael observed many children, some of darker complexion. A woman was inside with the children of various tender ages in her care.

"Come on up here," Michael said to Mrs. Ferree. "Look inside and see if one of these is the boy," Michael directed Mrs. Ferree who had closely followed him.

Mrs. Ferree climbed the portable stairs placed to the door of the wagon to look inside. "Yes, there he is!" Mrs. Ferree screamed in relief upon sighting the kidnapped child. She could not be restrained from opening the little half door into the shade of the wagon's inside to reach for the child.

A Gypsy woman inside did not try to prevent her. There would be no struggle. She came up to them as Mrs. Ferree clutched to herself Lamb's child. "He didn't look like he had no home," the woman said. "My boy said the child looked like it had been left out in the weather."

The woman looked tired. She was so thin. "We don't take babies," she insisted. "We have our own, but when a child don't have a home, we take in such. The stars give us this to do. We sweep the land of its children rejects and find them homes."

Mrs. Ferree was indignant. "We know how you people sell babies!" and grasped the baby so tightly that no one might ever dislodge the child again.

"Is the child in good state?" Michael asked of Mrs. Ferree.

Mrs. Ferree had taken Pleasant to inspect in each limb. "Yes, so far as I can tell," Mrs. Ferree replied.

"Not hurt!" the Gypsy woman insisted. "We do not hurt abandoned children, those unloved by the world. We take the homeless child and give them a home as God allows," she was saying in an imploring, gesticulated plea for understanding.

A man of the wagon had come upon the scene. Soon others arrived as well.

Michael waved his rifle to the crowd of men so as to indicate for them to part and permit him, Mrs. Ferree and the child to depart. The menacing group would not do so until Michael loosed a shot into the sky over their heads. "I expect that shot will be bringing some of the neighbor men, here, so I wouldn't want there to be trouble when they arrive." Michael took the precaution of re-cocking his rifle, eyeing the Gypsy men who had gathered around the wagon he had just searched. All the Gypsy men wielded a weapon of some sort. But they did back off to permit, Michael and Mrs. Ferree and the child to make their way through them.

The same group followed behind as Michael inched his way to the horse, mounted it, and shouted to the crowd, "Now we are going to leave here, and we don't want any following." "Back away!" The Gypsies did so and returned, most returning to their campfire within the circle of wagons, its huge iron pots steaming, others to their wagons.

After he mounted, Michael took the baby in his free hand, still with his finger on the trigger of his rifle in the other hand, while Mrs. Ferree was swinging herself up behind him.

For a first moment in time, Michael held the baby boy and brought him close to look at it. The little boy's weight was as laughter and tears. Michael's eyes beheld the child with a start! The torment of his life returned to him. This little baby had the eyes of Lamb Hackleman!

Why did she have to haunt his every move?

How could this child have the eyes of Lamb Hackleman?

Despite his rough appearing outer demeanor, in his chest Michael's heart was breaking as he saw this baby, whispering there from his soul in unspoken words to the baby how much he wished the baby was his very own and yet dreaming too of Lamb Hackleman whose eyes this child seemed to have. Must his life ever be lived in the illusion of his life and love of Lamb Hackleman now fading so quickly into the past?

Michael rode out of the camp at a gallop.

He would take the woman and the child to their homes in Oklahoma, outside Greenfield.

On the way back to the Gas Boom workers' camp, Michael thrust his rifle back in its hold and turned to ask, "Whose child did you say is the baby? Oh, yes," he recalled, "a mill girl you said. But what is the child's name?" Michael asked.

"Pleasant," came the reply.

Michael enquired further, "And who is the father?"

"He don't have one of them," the woman said.

This word silenced him and then the news boiled within him even more. Here a child without a father when he himself would have given the stars to have a child such as this brave and courageous boy. This boy, this child with Lamb's eyes, was a hero and Michael felt so proud of him. The child had never even cried during the crime. Michael felt so drawn to this fatherless child as if there had been some crossing of the stars which had caused him to be there to save him from being taken to another place and sold.

At Oklahoma, Michael took Mrs. Ferree's directions toward the shanty where the afternoon found no one else present outside. Michael again was given the child to hold as Mrs. Ferree dismounted, almost falling off the horse, and she then took the child back into her arms.

Michael could hardly bring himself to leave the little unfamiliar boy. Pleasant's helpless innocence stayed on Michael's mind. How he would like to have been the child's father. He would have cradled the child in the warm nights, sung him to sleep with the Deutsch lullabies of his forebears, and given him love beyond bounds. At a crazy moment he even dared to think how he might have been a father of such a child and Lamb the mother, if the world had been given over to permit such a miracle.

"Would the mother have any need of his aid?" Michael enquired of Mrs. Ferree. "No, she makes more than adequate provision," Mrs. Ferree said and went into the home after thanking Michael one final time.

For a moment, Michael could only fall into a dream. There had been something about this child, this boy who he had cradled in his arms. What was it? How could it be that he could see the features of his beloved Lamb in this child? He must be mad! Must Michael always see the features of Lamb in everything? She was as a ghost reappearing even in this child? Would that she be dead! Perhaps then, if she had any pity for one left without love and hope, she might then come to him as a specter and grant him the relief of her presence even if she would not consent, since her departure, to be with him in the flesh.

Michael's mind had tried to register how Lamb, if she had loved him, could have left without saying good-bye. And yet, he could not think of Lamb without remembering how they had lived and loved within each other's hearts in the lair of the Wild Bull of Blue River. Lamb remained there in Michael's heart. He could not leave this part of his heart behind. He could not live without Lamb's love. He would put his life behind him, all of it, if he should lose this part of Lamb which remained in his heart.

The little boy who looked so like Lamb also now was tormenting him, staying with him though left behind. Where could Michael go, where in all the earth, on what voyage by train or ship, that he might not be haunted by Lamb and her love. Why did he have to live now that she was gone?

Michael rode back down the National Road toward his home. His mind was blown by the sight of the boy who looked so like Lamb.

Going to town to turn in the Gypsies as kidnappers would have done no good. He knew very well that by the time the sheriff would get out to where the Gypsies had encamped they would be gone.

This trip had been a nightmare. He had not gotten Lamb off his mind at all, he had only found a child with her eyes who now deepened it. And yet, as he rode home, he thought to himself, how he had loved holding that child with Lamb's eyes. He wished he had recalled the child's name. Had this hysterical woman called his name Pleasant??? How he wondered if he would ever see the child again and yet he knew it would be impossible.

If he had only known what despair Lamb would cause him, would he have fallen in love with her anyway? Yes, came the answer from the depths of his heart. He had only been born to love Lamb Hackleman with a love which was lost in time. Why had there been no chance for the dream of a life with Lamb? What good is a dream anyway! It had only turned him into a fool!

14

Anna's Death

And now came November, the most miserable of months in the Hoosier Deutschlands and the time when nature dies.

As the days and months had moved forward with heavy steps, Anna could find less and less energy or desire to leave Lamb's childhood room in the Hackleman farm home. The tasks of arrangement and rearrangement of the room anticipating Lamb's return had ended now. Dust was gathering on the doll houses which had grown from one to two and then many. The little ceramic doll figures, with the hand sewn doll clothes, stayed within their tiny houses, none feeling the touch of the little girl who Anna was so sure was Lamb's child and her grandchild. The cradle with sheet now dusty had been pushed to the side. There would be no happy creaking from its rocking.

Anna's mind had begun playing vicious tricks upon her. That summer as she might toil in her garden trying to cause this little plot of the Hoosier Deutschlands to bloom, Lo and Behold! her soul would fly off in the company of a strange angel snagging her dress and forcing her to take wing to the East, where she could offer to bring her child home and then begin a laugh which would shake the world. It did no good to beg this angel to allow her to bring her child back to her, yes, Lamb, as still a child, and Lamb brought back to her arms, where her baby might not be buffeted by the world, and the uncertainties as life teemingly provides. The angel's laughs were as bells tolling. No? this could not be and so she would make a further demand, "Killer angel, you must destroy this world!" But that too was denied her until in her thoughts there came winged destruction which divided itself into four and each picking up a corner of her world, lifted up the earth's surface as a sheet for washing, and carried it off to oblivion. But it was a personal oblivion and it demanded that she confine her life to Lamb's room in the Hackleman home and no longer leave this place where she and Lamb had laughed and done the things that a mother does with her little girl in the undemanding trust that a mother and daughter share. The memory of her life with her beloved daughter was all that could save her from oblivion and this love she had driven away.

The fall had come and was nearly gone. Anna had stopped going into town. The family needed so little anyway that what was the use. Lemuel had willingly provided all the support he could. He knew that his wife was suffering of a broken heart, a depression which was as a bog drawing all of the joy of her life into its mud for sinking, but he could do nothing.

He could suggest that she remove her demand that Lamb's lover be prosecuted, that he was sure Lamb might return home, if only Anna would relent. Anna would hear nothing of it. Her heart was as a stone or rock. She would restore her daughter's reputation in the only way she knew it could be restored, by the bringing down of fiery retribution upon the loose morals of the boy who had ruined Lamb. She would redeem the little fatherless child that would be the burden these days of her daughter even if it meant her death. How she would wish to touch this grandchild!

So now floating, unresisting, falling, silently, unhasting, airlessly, as does music gently descending, slipping down through the Hoosier Autumn sky comes the red moment of dying heat bringing with her the healing hand of dark death. Up ahead was the woman who could not live longer in the truth of events. Death was as an arrow seeking Anna's broken heart.

Anna, trust the darkness. You cannot resist the night. The beat of your broken heart fades gently and slowly so that death can enfold you in its mystery. Feel it as a sweet intoxication to your soul, comforting, relieving, freeing you from the days. There, there. The fear loses its grip. The truth is nothing you could see in this world. Imagine the eternity of life in another realm. Eternity forgives. It wraps even the unforgiving in a mantle of aid. Charity holds you as your awarenesses silently flee and abandon their defenses.

The Angel of Mercy smiled tenderly upon Anna to relieve her of the burden of her breath. Your breathing leaves you so thankfully without wrenching. It was too great a burden.

Do you see her now, Anna, as your breath slips away, as the ember of your life burns out? It is your daughter Lamb impossibly coming to you from wherever she is, from whatever hell you have cast her into with your moralizing demands. Lamb holds you tightly, mother, her guiltless hands reach for your tearful cheek so thankful for this reunion in this last journey of yours to the light. Feel her hand on your cheek. She loves you still and would accompany you to wherever it is you go. She is telling you she will always think of you kindly for she loves you now as she always did and will despite every power of separation. There is nothing that can separate you from any love of your life, only the hates, the disappointments, the impossibilities.

Rest now, Anna, for you need no longer pretend a life that cannot be. You are dead now, your heart could no longer beat and drag on the miserable minutes, hours, and days. The truth is as it must be now and forevermore. You need no longer pretend that your daughter Lamb will return to you in life. Life was not as it ought to be. You could not will it otherwise. Accept the caress of Lamb who wishes you peace beyond life and its alienation.

It was on a Monday morning in October, as the leaves were dipping down from the trees, blown in confusion by the winds, that Lemuel found Anna dead in Lamb's room in the early morning as he rose to begin his day of solitude. Anna had not been his companion these last days. Her life had been drawn into another world from which she could not be shaken. It had taken her life. She could not accept the beginning of yet another week without relief.

Lemuel could only go outside, out into the heavy late fall air and shout out a lamentation that echoed into eternity. The crying did not cease until it echoed throughout the Blue River lands of the Wild Bull.

The wind tore and subdivided the sky into sheets of clouds. Sometimes the windy swirl appeared as a dark gray wave flowing downward in an uneven tide. Further away at a distance unfathomable were the whiter masses of air, also in windy confusion, but seeming to hug the ground all the way to the horizon. The brightness of the blue sky appeared only in hints of scribbles as in a language indecipherable and of mystery. What message, what parable, what prophecy, could such scribbles tell? The sun offered no illumination to the windy secrets.

Where does peace fly? And upon what wing?

Lemuel's cries into this windy air ended after a time.

There was only one thing that Lemuel could think to do. He would do his work. It had been his way, his ethic, his life.

He walked out to his barn in the drawing-down autumn afternoon and selected his sharpest squared spade for digging dirt. It wasn't in him to delay his work when work had to be done. He threw the spade over his shoulder and saddled up his horse. There was work to do and his Hoosier Deutsch blood gave him to do it while it was to be done.

Lemuel tightened the girth to his saddle, reached for its horn to drag himself up and reined his horse down the lane which led out to the county road from the Hackleman farm, turned to the East to the corner of the next road, where the trees were knotted on a knoll and their shade would offer some slight relief from the glaring truth of the sun. The air was heavy with the light it had shouldered all that day. The atmosphere seems to heave and sigh after the daylight hours begin to wane.

The white slab markers of a small country cemetery came into view as Lemuel tethered his horse and handled his spade. He had arrived at Gilboa Cemetery.

He entered the little cemetery on the ridge, separated from the world by only a small fragile black wrought iron fence and swinging gates over which Gilboa Cemetery were written. Its spine was a copse of chestnut and oaks.

He knew the spot to go to very well. It was an empty space next to another which contained two burial stones, marked with imprinted lettering on prior occasions, limestone slabs which had lost the imprint of most of that careful lettering and the family hex of a circular sun burst. All that could be read was the family name, Hackleman, on one of the time-scared stones.

Sadly Lemuel stood at the foot of his parents' graves.

Two spots, next to Lemuel's father and mother, had already been selected 40 years before, where Lemuel might rest with his wife. The spot for his anticipated wife was where he and Anna had always known it would be. That was the spot where Lemuel commenced his dig.

The ground was hard and objected to the intrusion. The season was sapping all its life. It was as if the soil itself resisted the obvious requirement that it receive the remains of this unwelcome seed of Anna Hackleman.

But Lemuel must persevere.

The other markers and silent stones in the cemetery witnessed his work. Their few names were predominantly Deutsch but some were of other national derivation.

Lemuel found relief in his work. It was good to do this, Lemuel thought to himself. It is something that must be done. The dry clods, with desperate nodules clinging to the grassy roots, began to respond to spade.

Soon Lemuel lost himself and his thoughts in his labors, digging his wife's grave, sweating, absent-mindedly, impassively. Lemuel hardly noticed it, when beside him appeared his young neighbor, Michael Sipe, who tapped him on his shoulder, and told him he would spell him for awhile.

Michael had heard the cries of the neighbor man howled into the autumn air and had gone to the home to discover the dead body of Anna lying in Lamb's room when no call came from his knocking. What a scene he observed there. Cobwebs and piles of baby clothes, doll houses and cabinets full of dolls. And then as he had gone out into the colding day he had seen Lemuel turning at the road toward the cemetery. Michael rode his horse at a gallop to find Lemuel digging. He would offer this beset man from the bereaved home whatever relief was in him to give.

The presence of another was a surprise which caused Lemuel's eyes to brow. He at first did not understand this relief offeror. His mind had been so engaged in concentration in the labors. But then, with a weak smile, Lemuel recognized the boy of the next farm. He would accept this young man's help.

And it registered that this young fellow had wished to shoulder his burdens for the while. Yes, it seemed good to let the boy take over. Lemuel had been working his mind feverishly, his body fevering, both beyond capacity, and he felt so heavy, detached from who he was, so different because halved by the death of his wife, operating in such a changed world since the short time before.

The cemetery was so still. It was nice to have the comforting presence of Michael Sipe with him. But more comforting still was the closeness to the dust of his parents and theirs. Would they understand his grief? Had his Deutsch ancestor's restless wanderings for a home on a new continent come to this! In his mind came the demons of estrangement death and ignorance to wreck the temple of his life. Before him was only the homelessness of a country grave to rot in! Lemuel went over to a huge blue beech and sat with his back to its trunk and rested under its shady but restive sawtooth leaves. He wanted to do something about his situation but there was nothing that he could do except to kick at the Virginia creepers and trumpet vines surrounding the tree with the heel of his boot. Even this slight act was as a disturbance of earthly order and its jar frightened and scared off a pair of cedar waxwings dressed in their blue and white and yellow tipped tails. His very presence was as an alienation, even in the place of death!

Would he no longer have any worth to anybody? Would he henceforth only intrude upon the lives of others and scare everything away with his mourning?

When the young man, Michael Sipe, had finished digging the grave to its proper depth of his own six foot height, the task he saw set before him, Michael went over to the bereaved elder neighbor, and helped him up.

Lemuel looked at the young man through tired eyes. He tried to brush away the young man's help. He could get by. Hadn't he always been strong! But he felt weak and closing his eyes, he melted, his limbs losing their muscle and bone, and for what seemed only a second, but for several minutes he fell into the strong posture of Michael's embrace, being supported in drear airless space. His head fell on the young man's shoulder brushing against Michael's stubbly cheek. Lemuel tried to cry without success. His body could only shudder and jerk. After this eternity of failed emotionality, Lemuel revived sufficiently for Michael to take him back to his horse. Michael would follow his neighbor home.

Only one further errand would Lemuel ask of this boy. Lemuel would seal up the news of Anna's death in an envelope and have Michael deliver the letter to the Greenfield paper mill so that Lamb might learn of her mother's untimely death. He addressed the letter "To Mr. W.H.H. Rock, mill officer." Surely Mr. Rock would see to it that Lamb would obtain the letter. If it had been addressed directly to Lamb from him, Lemuel feared she might not open it. Lemuel did not tell Michael the letter was for Lamb. He told him only that it was most urgently to be delivered. Michael saw the man in no fit state to answer further questions about the errand or to satisfy Michael's curiosity. Perhaps Lemuel saw the need to seek a crop advance to pay for the funeral or invite business friends at the mill to the interment.

Would Lamb find the regard to respond to the letter? There had been no time on this earth or its life for any final reconciliation by other estranged ones, mother and daughter. There was no earthly place where Anna might have one last long and imploring talk with her daughter. Perhaps the daughter might mourn her nevertheless.

Michael Sipe would gladly do this one further service. He mounted Red and rode toward Greenfield and the paper mill. The trip was quiet and quick as Michael walked up to the office of the paper mill and presented the sealed letter for the opening of the mill officer. Unbeknownst to Michael, it read, "Please inform Lamb Hackleman her mother has gone to her rest. The funeral is in the morning at 10 in the home and burial at 2 tomorrow afternoon at Gilboa. Father."

After the letter's delivery, Michael re- mounted Red, and rode out through the mill at a walk eyeing the buildings he had not seen so closely before. So strangely he felt close to Lamb here!

It was almost lunch - the next day, and a day late - before Lamb had the letter handed to her. It had been received by Mr. Rock who sent it down through the levels of bureaucracy until it reached the lowest level of employees where Lamb labored.

How had she come to have this news? And how did her father know to reach her in this place of her laboring? Was the letter true?

Sadly, the funeral had already been held, if the letter's information was valid. Its time of occurrence was past. Lamb had missed the funeral of her mother but she determined with every resolve that she would not be absent from the burial which would begin only minutes away.

With barely a word to the mill girls with whom she worked, Lamb made her decision. She would go to the interment of her mother no matter if it meant the losing of her precious job, her sole support for her and her child in their poverty.

She quickly stole away behind the brick buildings to the office's buggy shed. She must find a horse to ride...and quickly. Walking was out of the question for it would take far too long to travel the many miles to the cemetery of interment. Inside the paper mill buggy shed would be the riding horse of her employer and the stockowner's representative, Mr. Rock himself, who ran the mill. His was the only horse that was out of view. She must take it for there would be no other way to reach her father's side for the burial of her mother. No one must see her commit this crime if she would have a chance to retain her job through this deception.

Inside was the stable of Mr. W.H.H. Rock himself. His horse was a Tennessee Walker, marked by white sox and white forehead, a "gentleman's horse" as many would call its breed, a horse bred for the wealthy and for show. The horse accepted the nearby saddle and rider without objection. And then with Lamb in charge and a crop she found nearby in hand, the horse was released to the air of the outside and given its head. Soon Lamb sped across the lengths of the Hoosier landscape on her employer's mount, a fancy horse, cantering as in a running, a quick and smooth gait, so much less jarring than the trot of most breeds. The horse was used to speedy races in paddocks and he took to the open road just that way, sensing the urgency of his rider's quest.

The Gilboa Cemetery was up ahead on its knoll and Lamb spotted it right off. Less happily she saw there as well the small knot of folk gathered at the place within where she had always known the Hackleman family burial plot was located.

Tethering her borrowed horse, she arrived in time only to hug her father and stand by him as the pallbearers were carrying the coffin to the grave from the black draped wagon pulled through the gate and halted for the unloading of its pale cargo. The casket was seeded within the ground and the minister, Brother Aultman, took his place beside the lowered scar of digging, giving the final words, "Wer in diesem dienstbar war der im kunftigen Jahre frei." The prayer closed, Brother Aultman took into his hand a small touch of freshly turned soil and scattered it into the open grave not yet filled in.

The wind turned the air into heavy masses. Sometimes the masses collected and in the swirls curled themselves into giant heads of flowers, white blooming as appear peonies in the Spring, suitable for funerary display, but these illusive flowers would blow themselves out in the hushing sound that the wind made in its quiet tirade against any order or stability within the heavens. Then the whiteness of the blooms would disappear in a sneak over a level to be re-conformed as by the energy of the early afternoon sun into some other transformation elsewhere. The wind was destructive and determined to rid itself of even its own airy structures and paint everything in a dull grey wash. It did not just confine itself to mutating the sky either. It also snapped at the trees and leafy growth at the cemetery causing everything with plant surface to recoil in avoidance. Only the blue shadowing around the grave markers did not waver under its fury.

Lamb turned to Lemuel and told him softly, "Father I must leave now, I cannot stay. I will forever hold your love like a thought of hope in my heart," she said and then rushed off.

Her sad duty done, Lamb must return in a rush to her place of employment.

And then with last farewell, the others of the funeral party began to slowly leave. All would soon be departed with only the men of the neighborhood, most posse men, remaining to fill in the grave and mound it over.

This crew of the men stood as a knot while the mourning walked by. So quickly, as Lamb made her quick escape, she had gone over to them to give them thanks.

She nodded to some who had been her friends as the men hung together. Only one of the burial crew could she not help but see in surprise - Michael Sipe, who returned her gaze. Was he calling to her? Yes, she thought she heard his greeting. His voice was so richly deep, masculine and full. It was as music tumbling and burrowing into her soul. She had missed this sound every night.

For only a moment their eyes met, he as he stood, shovel on shoulder, in secret anguish and in wonder if this could be the neighbor girl of the weeks of the spring of his life. Only their eyes affixed for a moment. This day offered not even the relief of slight courtesy or return greeting. Before anything could be said, Lamb had departed.

She must ride back to the mill on her "borrowed" mount quickly. To be late would mean her job. The late autumn sky changed again and now hung in fists of grey clouds, heavy appearing, and knuckled in brighter indentations, appearing ready to strike into the ground at any moment in a fury, not at Lemuel as he stood silently by the spot of the closed grave where Anna lay, but at the ground as does a boxer's fist poised in readiness to vent frustration and to bury its fury into an opponent's soft flesh.

And Lamb must return to her home in the exile of her heart.

And to Michael was left only the wonder of where Lamb had gone to - a train for a return to her new home in Hellam, Pennsylvania? Where was this place graced by the presence of the woman he would have given his life to love.

Now he would continue his work and complete the task at hand. Michael would complete the filling in of Anna's grave - the woman who, if she could have had her way, would have had him dead and buried for fathering her grandchild of which he knew nothing!

But to Lemuel, he must stay in this land of his mourning and where his roots were in the same earth in which his little Deutsch wife now lay.

Had there really been a time when Lemuel Hackleman had lived peaceably with his Anna?

Where had it gone! And where was his peace with his daughter. Only once had he seen his grandchild and then not by right, but instead as an act of pity by strangers!

Their lives had been scattered on the hills like sheep without a shepherd.

15

Coming Home Christmas

Someone, more brave than the other girls, had asked the mill girl's supervisor, Gustavus Crider, if they could have more time off this week than just Christmas Day. Eventually, he had looked at them incredulously as if to start to say, "What cheek!" Instead he merely smiled at their impudence with a mouth engulfed in a massive growth of mustache and beard that flowed down from beneath his nose in a cascade. His head was not so well endowed with hair and was flat at the top with mere thatch over the ear and no sideburns at all. The only cognizable features were his eyes which appeared as under a single line of eyebrows, but eyes which were capable of great excitement and fury if any of the girls required correction in their duties. His voice was deep and rich. He added, "The holidays are Christmas and no other day!" He went on to explain, "The holidays cannot interfere. People need boxes and paper in the winter as well as summer -and our hours are lessened by the short days. Mr. Rock will not allow his customers to be let down."

Christmas would be the only day off in the week for the mill girls.

Cook your pulp girls, you can cook your geese and turkeys on Christmas. The mill girls' holiday spice would be caustic soda for pulp.

But to Lamb Hackleman there seemed a personal demand tugging at her heart. It was suggested out of some strange fullness in time as by an angel, "Go home to your father on Christmas, your one day off of the year," the thought echoed in her mind.

As Christmas Eve was falling into night, Lamb left the mill and began her evening's journey back to her home in Oklahoma. As the sun slipped down further and further in the sky, black ink seemed to replace the wintry cold and breezy air, squeezing the breatheable ether out of it, and leaving only this ink above that not only blackened the sky but flowed down out of it onto the land turning everything sable and funerary as if the land were a tar.

Lamb's life was this way, a tarry mire.

Perhaps this suggestion out of time might offer some hope to draw herself out of the mire of her life.

Yes, she decided, I will go home on this Christmas. She would return to her childhood home with her child, too. She would see her father and perhaps reconcile her life at least with him.

Strangely, if her mother had not died, she would not have dared to return home. No such fruit could have been tasted. But her father, now that her mother was dead and buried, would be so lonely that her mother's ban from the homeplace lost its force. She would return because her mother's order for her exile was dead and buried with her, lost in another time and another reality now a situation at an end.

That night, Christmas Eve after work and after Lamb retired to her cot in the corner of the Ferree home, she took her child to her side, hearing the usual demand from this little beloved child, "Tell story." Well she would do that and also tell the boy that they would take a trip to her farm home the very next day no matter what.

Pleasant fidgeted while his eyes flirted with sleep. "Tell about the Wild Bull," Pleasant insisted.

"Pleasant," the tired woman said, "I will do so but then we must sleep." She would tell the boy the same story which she had told him so often.

"Once upon a time there was a Wild Bull in Indiana. It was a bull which loved people but was unloveable and folk did not love it back. The bull had to do what it had to do. It had a mission: to get people to love each other. It was loose because God wanted it to be ready to help people the minute they needed it. Its mane was red and fiery as the sun and its look through black eyes could scare away the Devil itself. One time a little boy got lost in the land. He did not know where to go. There was no one in the entire forest of the earth but hunters and killers of living things. Look, up ahead," she said. "There behind a tree is a hunter. He is wanting to kill anything that moves. Watch out, Pleasant. Bang!" she said, "giving the little boy a hug while he squealed with delight. Watch out, there he goes again, reloading. Watch out. The little boy looks like a rabbit, he does. Watch out, Pleasant."

The little boy snuggled close to Lamb as he often did at this part of the tale.

"But wait, up ahead, there is the Wild Bull," Lamb said. "Run to him as providence directs," she said. "And there he comes to drive away the hunter whose gun is ready to shoot the both of you! See Wild Bull's horns pointed at the deathdealer. One of them is called Thunder and the other Lightning. Wooosh, Wild Bull blows over the land and at the hunter like the wind. There goes the hunter," she said, running her finger down his chest. "The hunter has left. You must never fear the Wild Bull," she said very solemnly closing her eyes. "If you ever know trouble or fear, trust in the Wild Bull and follow where he leads. Trust in love." Then, her thoughts turning to dreams of the man whose love she still bore in her heart, she fell asleep.

When the early morning came, Lamb arose and looked down at her clothes. It was Tuesday, Christmas Day, and the day's work previous at the paper mill had not permitted her to come home before the darkening of the skies. With a cry she saw the tears and worn spots that no lye soaping could remove.

Then she looked at the small shelf where the clothes of her baby boy, Pleasant, were kept in a neat stack, or such as there were. It had been all she could do to find the rough coat outworn by a neighbor boy in Oklahoma for him to wear for the winter but it would do for this day of journeying. The roundabouts and pants seemed to make such a tiny stack in the morning light.

Oh, well. The day must not be wasted. It was just for the day that she would be free to go to her father's farm for Christmas. She dressed quickly and then dressed her sleepy child.

Pleasant was fussy but willing.

They would have only a few miles to walk to reach the farm home of her family upon Dilly Crick and she wished to arrive as early as possible for this one day of leisure.

Winter was upon the land evidenced by traces of white in strangely shaped globs and stretches along the fence rows and rocky outcroppings and back within the occasional stands of brush and trees upon the route. The red cones of the leafless bushes of sumac appeared as cold dry flames. Then upon the roofs of houses, barns and sheds too the snow was a covering. Apparently it survived only in the massing for otherwise the winter painted the land in browns and greys. Even the tree limbs showed no sign of white. The sky, still in light blue, nevertheless was clouding in the way that would mean another snow would come and more than likely this very day.

Lamb carried Pleasant in her arms for long stretches and then, from time to time, she would let him down. He was so close to two years of age that he could now walk for more extended distances. She would sometimes have to rush to catch up with him heedless to her scolding to stay along the side of the trace.

Rarely did she look far ahead on the road to know what her next mile might encounter. Only at the breaks in the fields or near the waterways where covered bridges sheltered an over-passage was there vantage to see ahead anyway. But what did it matter? She would allow the day to tell its own story. Soon they would be to the farmhouse where Christmas awaited.

She could imagine her father cutting down a Christmas tree for the parlor of the Hackleman home. Yes, he would cut the very largest tree he could find. She could imagine her father standing beside that tree and looking it over for branches that might need pruning. His face would be so long too. His expression became so merrily fastidious at times. He would love it when she came home if only her father could forgive her in his heart for having lived scandalously. Pleasant could help the lonely man place the gaily colored balls upon the tree and the ribbons and candles too!

That the two were so cold in their walk did not matter. It would not have mattered if the sun were out, or it rained, snowed, or sleeted, or hailed. They were going home for Christmas.

She would ask her father to forgive her fallen state. Her father could do no less than tell her to leave again.

Her poor Wild Bull, she thought, as the two, mother and son, reached the border of the Hackleman farm. He must have been almost starving by now. There would be no reprieve for him from the harshness of the weather. She had not seen him now for many weeks. She resolved to try to do so if she could only find the time in this one day only when she would be permitted to leave her work place. What if she could not return to her home at Oklahoma? The overhead clouds threatened at any moment to break out into a slight snow or blizzard, exactly what could not be predicted.

As Lamb, carrying Pleasant, approached the house up the long lane, Lemuel stood at the window. With a cry he saw the forms moving against the backdrop of snow. And then he recognized the form as being that of his daughter. It was Lamb come home for Christmas! And she had brought the boy. What a Christmas he would have. Could it be that life that had been so awfully wrong, could now become so providentially right? The father left the warmth of the house to go out to the lane and then down it with a whoop and a cry of welcome.

He would not hear any talk of the past. Her return needed neither be in triumph or despair. Soon the three were in a greeting hug that was as warm as the temperature outside was cold.

"Father," Lamb whispered in Lemuel's ear, "don't you have one word of anger at me for all the depth to which my life has sunk?"

"No, not one," he replied.

Her father's hug, sure and strong, convinced her she was spotless and pure. Lamb felt strengthened immediately. "And this is your grandchild," she told Lemuel, giving over the boy, now nearing two, to the arms of his grandparent. "His name is Pleasant." Lamb did not know that her father had once before held the child as a baby, but only once.

"Oh, Pleasant," the old man said, his eyes welling with tears to hold the child again. "How often it has been that I would hold you in my arms and could not!" The little boy was as a lump of clay squirming comfortably into this shape and that within the unfamiliar grasp of the old man.

Soon they were inside the home. Lamb breathed its air in joy all mere hope excelling.

"Oh, father," she cried out upon entering the home's warm front parlor, "Where is the Christmas tree? I was so sure one would be here in the front hall!"

"No, Lamb, I saw no need," the tired looking man replied.

"Then you shall go out and select one at once," she announced, taking her father by the hand. "Pleasant can go with you to pick."

There must be this flurry of activity for the day would be short.

Lemuel would do as he was told. Out behind the house was the barn pathway he would take with the child and they would go to the bank of the crick beneath the barn to a spot where a fir was in Lemuel's mind for a chopping.

Soon went the grandfather and his small grandboy out to fetch this fir for a Christmas tree. Lemuel kept the boy upon his arm out to the barn and then, armed with the ax, he and Pleasant walked the steps down to a cliffy area along the crick where a few evergreens sported. There were a few such precipitous places upon the course of the crick where even the cattle, usually sure-footed, did not go for forage. These were mainly the steeper areas where the waters were knifing into the bank during the heavy and wild spring rainy seasons. Here were scrubby trees without leaves that thrust up out of the soil waving their upper branches as hands seeking in vain for relief from the cold air. In this area was a fur tree which would do for the season's Christmas tree. Lemuel left Pleasant on a snowy shoulder between patches of leafless brush overlooking the crick while he found himself a stick for a balancing cane and straddled the steeper portion of this isolated place to come to the tree, cut it, and return. Lemuel's steps were far livelier than he had ever dreamed they might be this day. He would be glad to return to the warm house for the sky above was white, unevenly moving in the agitation of holding far too much snow, and threatening blizzard.

In the meantime, Lamb would go to her mother's kitchen and see if a Christmas meal might be prepared. Here was the kitchen just as she had remembered it from the many months before - its rough-hewn kitchen table where she had sat so pleasantly as a child. She smiled to think of standing on the stenciled kitchen floor as she had in other, younger years. There were the cabinets, buttermilk painted, and she went to open them and look inside to see the dark blue and green glassware and plates. The tall free standing cabinet still had the earthenware pots on them placed high for they were not for Lamb to touch as a girl. Pegs near the ceiling contained so many of the kitchen utensils that Anna had wielded in her happier days.

When Lamb opened the door to her girlhood bedroom she let out a cry. She had expected to see merely the ancient patch quilt upon her bed, but here was more, so much more. What had her mother done! Stacks of baby clothes and racks of hand stitched items, dolls and toys abounded. Lamb recognized then the hours that her mother must have spent in Lamb's former room before her death. Hours and hours of work for a child were within inventory. Lamb selected a few toys for later placement under the Christmas tree. She would do this for her mother. Anna had worked diligently to provide for her grandchild and Lamb would see that this labor was applied to its purpose. The room was a confirmation of what Lamb had always known in the secret places of her heart -that her mother had loved her and her grandchild very deeply. Now Lamb knew how tragically her mother had suffered her loss before her death. Yet, that she was now returned on this Christmas Day seemed somehow its healing.

Soon Lamb's father was back with a Christmas tree on his shoulder. Pleasant was an armload on the other shoulder. They would set the tree up in the front parlor and soon the tree was in place, dressed in its trinkets and festoonings.

"Oh, father," she said, "We shall make this a joyous day. I shall purchase a yuletide goose. And I will prepare potato dumplings and mother's apple sauerkraut salad, and," she thought, "yes, a creamy raisin pie for dessert."

She went out into the kitchen to make a quick grocery list. She would need the goose, bay leaves, prunes, basil, oranges, and apples for the stuffing too!

She must make a quick trip into town. That was obvious. Lemuel offered the quicker transportation of Anna's buggy.

Then, without time to waste, Lemuel went out with Lamb to the barn to see to it, this transportation, to hitch up the sorrel, and see his sorely missed daughter off to Fisk's Meat Market on the town square in Greenfield. She must hurry for it closed at noon on Christmas Day. She must also hurry because the weather threatened a heavy snow.

Lamb took her departure. As she left Lamb looked upward toward the heavens. What weather would such a day bring about? The clouds were still growing heavier and heavier and filling the sky, turning the air white and misty. Snow was beginning to fall, a snow which began immediately to deprive the land of its contours and blanket it with white as if to purify it and hide its glitches and erosions. Already there was a fresh salting of snow on the ground even after the short time before when she and Pleasant had walked from Greenfield out to the farm. Then the day had been bright with morning. Now the weather seemed changing and the landscape appeared as a dreamy white. Tiny white flecks were falling distract- edly, confusing the scene in metamorphosis. The particles were the kind which melt on your clothing before they can be brushed off. Her horse sloshed in the snow down the lane because the tempera- ture was not yet so cold as turns the snow into something crinkly. This snow was wetter and formed lumps and then deliquescence where it accumulated on the road. Its thaw caused small streams to appear beside the route as Lamb travelled into town and the snow was soon rippling shallowly there. Elsewhere, on the land and fields, the snow did not melt so easily. Much nastier weather offered to soon appear.

After Lamb left, with Pleasant in his care, Lemuel puzzled how to entertain his grandson. The snow gave him the idea for a play with the child. Yes, that would be fun. A romp in the snow would be his to enjoy with his grandchild. He might take the child outside to play in the snow in the front of the home and where the farm's hillocks began their descent to the lower meadows.

There could never be danger in a play in the snow.

16

A Lost Boy

The surprise Christmas visit by his daughter had turned Lemuel's Christmas day into a holiday.

Lemuel could not wait to share the farm and the mysterious snow with his grandson. What fun they would have! The snow! Yes, they would go play in the snow. That would be such fun!!! The expectation of it rose in his mind, the feel of the snow's white slip and slide recollected from his own youth, the joy of its unexpectedness as a gift of providential clouds now beginning to unload in greater profusion, of the innocent pleasure of being in the snow's sloppiness and give.

He bundled Pleasant up in his coat for the air was turning colder as the snow really began to fall and fall. Lemuel then wrapped him in a warm scarf. Pleasant cooperated. He trusted this man, this friendly grandfather so newly injected into his life. Then they went outside.

Even in the short minutes since Lamb's departure, the snow had fallen to form new layers over the former patches. There were several inches of snow in the coming and a substantial amount already graced the ground.

First Lemuel and his grandson built a snowman, imagined it as a living creature with a smiling rocky mouth, in the front yard. Quite a feat! The new snow was wet and packed with ease.

There was so much to do. Grandpa says, "Let's make angels by lying down in the snow. Now, flap your arms in arcs through the snow!" Both grandpa and grandson did so. Soon the white lawn was filled with angels. The snow continued its fall.

"How about a snowball fight with grandpa!" Soon the two were aglow in the flinging snow, harmlessly pelting each other in exaggerated playful aggression.

But all of this activity was taking its toll on the old man. Lemuel was becoming breathless with the unexpected activity of this day. He would take a break from such feverish sport. He would go in and sit by the window for a minute on his favorite chair. "You stay out here and play a while if you want to," Lemuel had told his grandson. "Grandpa will watch you from the window for a minute."

The little boy was so engrossed in his play that he hardly heard him. There was the game of throw the snow ball at the trees. The amusement of falling down in soft comfort on the snowy lawn. The diversion of making piles of snow into castles.

Lemuel went inside. He sat himself down where he could see the little boy in his continuing fun in the snow, a spot where he often sat inside the front parlor observing the front portion of his farm. He knew his farm by the inch and his grandson could not find a place where he could not locate him. He would be safe while his grandfather rested from his overexertion.

Then, as Pleasant continued his sport over by the snowman in the front yard and then down toward the pond he noticed some cottontail kaninchenbau tracks that gave the appearance of the paw prints of a tiger or lion rather than a bunny. He went to observe them but without danger since the pond had been frozen over by the below freezing weather.

As Lemuel sat on his chair watching the boy, the shadows out-side danced and mesmerized him. He could not keep his eyes from taking in too much of this joyous farm dressed in snowy coat. It was the outside patterns of sunbeams on the still accumulating snow that were too intricate to follow that were causing him to lose focus and desire to rest his eyes. Perhaps it was the accustomed naps he took on this chair too which lulled his eyes to closing. He often would rest here with closed eyes in the long afternoons between his chores with the herd. Lemuel felt so comfortable and so happy that it worked upon him as an exhaustion that demanded that he close his eyes for a second before his daughter's return and while the child was at harmless play. The grandpa's eyes just would not stay awake and there was no watching going on as his grandson followed the bunny tracks out of the front yard.

The path was familiar from the short time earlier when the little boy had gone with his grandfather to find the Christmas tree behind the barn.

Then there were more tracks to be discovered. Following them around the hill the little boy heard a calf in the barn calling for its mother brood cow.

There is nothing more pitifully sad than a little calf wanting its mother brood cow. The little calf gathers itself up with a welling of breath hard to catch anyway until it lifts its head up, opens its mouth with its tongue pushing at its lower lip and bursts forth an urgent demand for attention.

The sound was so demanding that the little boy himself decided to go see if he could be of some help.

By the time Pleasant got to the barn the little calf had found its mother brood cow and the situation had returned to normal. But the situation wasn't normal to the little boy.

He had not seen his grandfather's cattle gathered in the barn before. These cows, so large and exciting to the little boy! They could be his pets for awhile!

Hadn't grandpa given him the run of the farm this day for his amusement?

After he had played in the barnyard for a little while, and played "pets" with the cattle, the little boy looked beyond. Dilly Crick was just down the hill. It was as if Dilly Crick was telling him "Go south, it is a road." There were the hay fields spread before him, but behind the barn was the slope down to Dilly Crick. Wasn't this the same place where he had gone with his grandpa to fetch the Christmas tree such a short time before? He would rest just a minute before going down there. Yes, the time was up, he would be on his way!

At the heights behind the barn a new thought beckoned. The little boy thought he might like to go down to the crick to investigate its situation to stay and move about it freely. The little crick had such a merry look, as its clear ripples, one by one, reached back to pull more of the mumbling water along.

Pleasant followed the cattle path down from the barn in his awkward childish-walking way to the gentle lapping crick, humming its way between icy rock outcrops, branch pileups and snags, and banks capped with filling snow. The crick was as clear as if the water were crystalline or perhaps illusory. He half way slid down the slope to this crick and then followed the meander that the path takes to snake its way from the barn to the ford where the crick bubbled and called him.

At the crick he noticed the pathways by its side going in either direction along its course and passage.

Cow paths are funny ways to follow, especially in entrancing snow. They are like a rut through the meadow, a mud dug indent into the clods of the grasses and sod. They were not intended for little boys to walk down them, but they did constitute a pathway that suggested to the little boy to follow to see where they came out.

After the little boy had thrown snow and ice into the laughing waters for a while to watch the splashes break into the air, he fell to the temptation to follow one of the southern-directed cow paths.

And as he would stop to observe the crick some more, he would notice how fascinating the crick looked further down where it flattened out into a sand bed before gathering to rush on through some heavy rocks. And beyond that there was a high bank of mud swelling down from a hill. Was there the bunny he had seen at the house? Something furry was in a rush to the bank! He would go see where the rabbit had disappeared to.

He found the spot and thought to investigate it, a nesting spot of cottontails, and found himself tripping on the shallow cratering nest lined with hair from the female. He caught himself as out of the kaninchenhohle the young rabbit darted.

These mysteries, and others, beckoned the little boy to wander further and it was not long before he had climbed over the border crick fence that separated the Hackleman farm from its neighbor place. The border fence wasn't that hard to negotiate. He could easily pull himself over and not have to rely upon any "lift" from some absent grandfather or mother!

Here the crick opened out more into a meadow where horses ran. Hay was in a stack here, made messy around its perimeter by the traffic of these horses to nibble into its bounty. He did not see them until down a ways and by the time they came over to him to see if he was bearing any oats or other interesting things, he had wandered as far down the crick as if he had been walking for at least an hour.

Horses were a different matter than the placid cattle. They were sleek animals with shiny coats and legs that stilted high up in the air. The snorting heavy breathings of them scared the little boy. Their pluming breaths were probably fire. Smoke was emerging as they approached and the little boy picked himself up a the rock to throw. He would go now down to the deepening waters.

Except that there appeared in front of him, almost from no where, the Wild Bull of Blue River obstructing his path to a death in the dangerously icy waters whose banks were so slippery.

When the little boy saw the beast up ahead, he did not feel any terror at all. The bull up ahead looked close to the way his grandfather's cattle looked. Was this the friendly bull of his mother's story of the night before and so many other nights? Pleasant decided to go and meet him.

The little boy did not know that the neighbors called the Wild Bull the devil himself. He did not know the Wild Bull was the killer of the neighborhood.

At first the Wild Bull stood its ground.

But the Wild Bull could not ignore the little boy coming up to him in his sanctuary.

The Wild Bull lowered its head so that the points of its steel tearing horns waved defiantly. But as if to gain a better perspective to see the little intruder closer up, he raised his head and then as he came even closer the Wild Bull sank to the ground with a huge thud and allowed the little boy to come close while the little boy petted and tugged at his main. This child was the one he had seen with his

Lamb on the Spring night when Lamb would come to seek relief from her days at the mill.

The Wild Bull rolled his eyes and as the little boy came around to touch his wet nose, the bull gave the little boy the wettest and happiest licks any little boy could have ever received.

These licks made the little boy giggle and laugh and the whole woods seemed to be lighted up by the sight of the huge beast and the little boy in play and joy.

Together the two would go investigate down crick. As the two continued their walk together, the Wild Bull made sure he was between the boy and these dangerous waters.

This more open meadow eventually, in the last stretch of crick, joined up with Blue River itself, river of the wider expanse and carrier of the levels of the icy waters of the land. The falling heavy snow continued to fill the area.

Its woods was not hard to travel through. The winter had killed off the leaves, shattered and crushed them.

Here, along the snowy banks of Blue River, the boy saw the most beautiful rock in the world. It was all he could do at his tender age, just two, to pick it up. He did so. Now what. But where to throw it?

Pleasant would go to the river to pitch it in. He arched it high into the air and when it landed it broke through the ice. And then sounded the plunk that a rock makes when it meets water. Now Pleasant would go see what damage he had done. He would walk out to where his rock had broken the ice to see what had happened. The Wild Bull could not stop him.

At the river, Pleasant took notice of his situation. The crack his rock had made in the river was out a ways. The boy tested the sand in front of him. It seemed steady enough. Yes, the frozen sand bar beneath his weight would support him very well. But then, not far out, the sand bar ended and a sheet of ice began, a sheet which covered the river. His rock crater was just a bit further out.

Out in front of the boy was only an ice shelf. Pleasant thought it quite sturdy enough to hold him. He had a little further out in the river to go in his investigation.

The blizzard was really making the stepping very difficult along the bank anyway.

Just another few inches was the hole in the ice where the rock had plunged.

And then Pleasant was out on the river ice and at the hole. When he looked in imagine his surprise. There was a boy there. How would he have known it was his reflection. No, it was a boy in the river who was making faces at him and wanting him to play just as he himself felt right then.

Well, he would play too and if the boy in there was safe why wouldn't he be safe in the river too?

In an instant, Pleasant had slipped into the depths of the icy river and under the shelf of ice above. Immediately his eyes grew big and he felt terror looking up and seeing nothing but water and trying to breath and finding no air for breath.

His hands began to reach for something, anything, to hold onto. There was nothing not slippery and freezing. The gulps for air were not working either. Only water seemed to be coming into his throat. He wished to cry out for his mother, Lamb, to come to his assistance as he did when in distress. There was no breath in his lungs to cry out. His vision began to fade into a blur.

It could have been forever but was only an instant.

Another splash and another life had broken through the ice to reach Pleasant. It was the Wild Bull of Blue River.

The Wild Bull thrust his head under the ice and waved his head in a search. Ahead everything seemed blue and brown. With a crash he withdrew his head up through the ice to take a breath and blow away the watery coat over his nose. Then he dipped his head under again. There ahead was the boy, drawn by a strong undercurrent to the river's bottom, being carried along the shoreline. He would reach the boy through the barrier of ice like glass which crinkled and cracked and cut as he burst along the shoreline to where the boy was.

And with a dip of his horn he caught Pleasant's coat and pulling it behind he struggled up the icy bank breaking the stinging and rending ice until he was on shore with the boy.

Pleasant was silent and then, coughing, found air again to breath. Soon his cries filled the air until the Wild Bull rubbed and licked at his face and settled himself about the boy with a thud, setting himself up to intervene in the buffeting of the snowing storm. It was no use trying to nose the boy to shelter beyond in the woods. The boy could no longer move. The Wild Bull would have to give his own body warmth for shelter for now. Here the boy, cold and spent, stayed until his eyes closed fitfully in exhaustion.

And the afternoon tolled as the little boy slowly began to freeze to death in his wet clothes.

When the grandfather woke up - was it an hour later? -or into the second hour? Lemuel looked around the darkened parlor and realized much time had passed. What had he done? He had fallen asleep and left his little grandson alone and out playing in the snow in front of his house. As he looked out he saw the snow falling in huge profusions.

A blizzard had begun. Lamb would be much delayed in her return from town.

He stood up before the window to look out but he could hardly see out at all. Where he could observe, he could not see the child. The little boy was not there. Nor could he see him - or any sign of him - in the wide expanse out over the fields and hills to the front of the farm home.

He thumped and thumped at the window to arouse the notice of the little boy if he had been hiding. But there was no response.

Throwing on his coat in a great rush, he ran out into the snowy scene. In ever increasing fear, he searched frantically, calling out, "Pleasant, Pleasant." But there was sorrowfully no answer.

And then began the blizzard in his soul. What if the child were dead and lying somewhere beneath these building mounds of snow rising now to inches. With great fright he kicked at the mounds that he could see. None yielded flesh.

Then the old man saw the filling tracks of a boy's walk. To find him alive would require a miracle. The tracks led around the hill the house was situated on. There was only the one thing to do, to follow those steps in the deep snow to their destination whatever destination that might be.

Lemuel set out tracking his grandson. The footsteps led around the house and around the crest of its hill, toward the barn. Lemuel called for Pleasant with voice that soon lost its ring in desperate hoarseness. The old man called and called into the heavy air.

At times the tracks could not be followed but would reappear providentially. The footsteps stopped near the barn which the old man entered through its wide doors. Could he find some sign of the little boy? Again the calls went unanswered. Could Pleasant have climbed the splintery ladders to the loft? The old man climbed up to see if the child was observable there. Head high into the hay mow, he could see enough and there was no sign of the little boy in the midst of the hay piled up to the open beams of the roof. A hoarse call brought forth no response.

Returning to the ground floor, Lemuel opened a stall and looked into others now empty fearing Pleasant might have fallen asleep in one of them. The he investigated the forschuss. What must have been an eight foot black rat snake, blotched with yellow, scurried from its shadows. Something had been constricted laying in its corner, Lemuel could not tell what. His imagination wanted him to say that the shadow could have been Pleasant but closer examination found it to be something else - the remains of an opossum with its tail as that of a rat?

He moved as quickly as he could to look elsewhere. But his fear for the little boy led him to feel as if his movements took forever. He might as well have been in slow motion. A pair of barn owls, their wings flapping, soared out as Lemuel banged at the wood of the structure with a board to arouse whatever could be aroused.

Lemuel feared the worst and looked among the herd. Could Pleasant have been knocked down or stepped onto unconsciousness in the path of one of the cows. The thought froze the man. Again, his shouting, resulted in nothing. There was no sign of the little boy anywhere in the barnyard and Pleasant did not answer his calls, as loudly as he could give them.

Lemuel frantically began to search the periphery of the barn lot. Then it occurred to him that maybe he might see the boy, despite the heavy falling snow, from the highest point to the rear of the barn. He went to the back of the barn in a rush. Here he could observe the whole section of Dilly Crick laid out below. His scan was fruitless. He called out but heard only the return of vacant echoes.

He went to the path leading down to Dilly Crick and its course with eyes gawking to find even the slightest sign of his grandson. Yes, as if by a miracle, there was another footprint of a child, quickly filling with the heavy snows. The glowing snow was threatening to blind him from seeing more. The boy had wandered down into the crick meadow!

His daughter Lamb might be returning any time. It seemed many precious minutes had passed and noon was the time. Under the building snow which blinded it out, the sun by now must have reached its nadir in the sky.

With the blizzard intensifying, Lemuel realized it would be hopeless for himself alone to find the child in the snow filling meadows along the crick ahead. The many directions the child might have gone were beyond his sole means to search. What if he had reached the heavy woods to the south where Blue River flows? His quick glance at that direction brought into view the 200 foot sycamores whitening as the grew until their tops, as the white hair of old men, showed their age.

One last hopeless effort he might make by himself. He would search the short stretch of Dilly Crick at the foot of the barn path near the ford below. While the bank was yet building into huge drifts, he went down its path to the crick. Again his calling out the name Pleasant was in vain.

Up and down this short stretch he shuffled, looking both around the meadow and into the crick in a desperate effort to see if the child might have fallen in.

There, not far to the south in the crick, he thought he saw a form under a snow which cast a mantle on an icy form. Lemuel would go out in the crick to it thinking it might be his grandson.

Striding and splashing in the crick, he felt the freezing water enter his boot. No, the object was nothing more than a jam of sticks at a rock.

Lemuel would have walked the crick further but he saw coming at him a snapping turtle which looked to offer a fight. This one was over a foot in length, weighing close to 50 pounds, and had only one eye, probably the result of a past battle. It can bite off a toe through thick leather in a lightning snap. Lemuel could hardly see it there coming along the crick bank and yet he would back off and avoid it. But what if Pleasant had encountered this monster? Had he lost an arm or leg to this very creature - looking so voracious, its open jaws asking Lemuel just to try coming closer?

There was no seeing even further than a foot or two ahead as the snow continued its descent in piling clouds. The disheartened and desperate man, hiding the world's saddest heart, must give up his search. Neither he nor the saints in Jerusalem could have done the finding individually.

Lemuel made his way back up the hill, his thoughts heavier still. He must go for help.

Why could not his steps have sunk him down into an escaping welcomed grave? How much rather he would have found himself dead and buried than to have to face his dereliction, his carelessness about his grandson and his safety! The fault should have been with the earth in failing to open up and receive him, the case against him was so clear and damning. Fault should have tasted him, drawing his very being into its sentencing maw.

He recalled some of the neighbors claiming they had heard a pack of coyotes were running close by. When had that been - this week? The week before? Last month? His tormented mind was lost in trying to remember a little noted piece of neighborhood gossip. Would they be rabid?

He knew of no way to follow the boy into the wilds of the Blue River woods by himself in this extent of blizzard.

Beings above! Please chant a song of comfort to this man. Rebecca? Reveal to this man his child - where lies his concealed treasure, his grandchild so innocent and vulnerable to the storm of life!

The most danger of all, from the Wild Bull, centered his fear and caused all other apprehension and horror to pale. Why had he not himself gone off to hunt down and kill the Wild Bull before now? He had not taken seriously enough this threat. He should have killed this deadly force! Even now, the Wild Bull was threatening or child murdering his grandson. Why had God given life to him whose way was hidden, whom God had hedged in? If his grandson, Pleasant, were to die he would be responsible for it, as surely as if he murdered Pleasant himself? Guilt seemed to attach so firmly sealing him in its sick indictment. Was it not enough that he had broken his covenant with Lamb to watch her son?

"Pleasant is lost," the old man had to tell himself with the thickest tongue a grandfather ever used in communication. "Pleasant is lost!"

There was only one thing to do. Quickly the old man went to the barn and saddled his horse to go to the neighbor farm to solicit help from Michael Sipe. The posse would have to be called out and quickly.

Galloping to the neighbor farm in a flash, Lemuel told the young neighbor man, Michael Sipe, the news. Together the two rode out to inform others close by. Soon all must gather at the Hackleman farm if the child described by Lemuel Hackleman might have a chance to live.

Were there snowy mountains in the sky this day? The blizzard had turned the sky into visions of white mountains. One could not tell more because the snow clouds made angular intrusions through the air shaping it into what might have been slopes upward with the blueness of their airy partners the color of distant snowy ranges. Then this strange, illusive air would change so that up above was a blanket of grey, changing again into a swirling display of fanning wisps. The sky itself was as a tiding that change was in the air. Would it token a change in every life? Or lead to Pleasant's death?

Soon the horse thief protection company would gather at Lemuel's barn to assist in the search. It did not matter whether it was Christmas Day or not.

Lemuel returned to his farm for the wait. And now there came time for patience and waiting for the search to proceed, when patience would not come. There was nothing he could rail against nor did Lemuel shake his fist at God and vaunt himself against the Almighty. He tried to comfort himself as he could by repeating that to God belonged wisdom and power. Counsel and understanding are His. But in the end he could only find the words to say, "My God! MY God!" The terrible realization that his grandson might have met death on the Wild Bull's terrible horns flew at him as if carried in a whirr by terrible wings. In the blizzard could be imagined the faces and livery of the horsemen of the apocalypse.

Finally out of a time that had stood still, here came the posse. Most had their guns loaded claiming that the Wild Bull might be on the loose. They then took off on their reluctant horses taking the paths behind barn, across ford, and down the crick paths on a search of the meadows and the river beyond for the small child.

Michael stayed with Lemuel upon hearing that Lamb would soon be there to explain further.

"Whose child is it," Michael asked.

"It is Lamb's."

"And what is the child's name?"

"Pleasant," Lemuel told him.

"Pleasant?" Michael asked again incredulously. He had once cradled a boy he had rescued from the Gypsies by that name. Could that child have been Lamb's?

"And the age of the child?" Michael asked.

"Almost two years," Lemuel answered.

Michael's mind was becoming boggled. If the child were Lamb's and of that age, could the child Pleasant have been his?

The sky was becoming a rolling thunder of white snow.

Michael knew now more than he could have expected to know. This lost child could be - or was it - his - a child he had never known except in a providential moment.

And here came Lamb rushing up from the buggy parked without tether in the drive. She had seen the many tracks of horses on the land and knew a hurried gathering was at the rear of the lane. The blizzard quietly tried to hide her from the terror of the landscape where her son was lost beyond her father's, Lemuel's, retrieving.

17

Christmas Family Reunion

Lamb rushed to her father. "Why are all these men present here at our home," she asked Lemuel. Her father seemed in such despair. He was a storm tossed man who no longer had the strength to wander alone in the searching for his grandson. Then Lamb turned to the neighbor boy Michael Sipe. Her surprise was complete. "Michael, why are you here? Why does this Christmas not find you at home?"

"I came after gathering the posse," he replied, looking at Lamb so filled with emotion over the strange news that Lamb had borne a son. "Your father called us to assist him." Why did his heart beat as if it were coming alive?

Lamb again looked at her father in fright.

"Is something wrong with the child?" she asked. Lemuel recounted the morning and how the child was now lost. He tried to be matter of fact about the incident with his daughter as he had been with the neighborhood posse leader. He tried to be clear and plain, in his usual manner, about details. But it was hard for him to restrain the grief that was so deep in him. Despair pooled his eyes.

Lamb was left to the terror of her life - the loss of her child. "I am here to help, Lamb," Michael said. "I had not known you were a mother." Lemuel alone did not understand how desperate that caused Michael to feel. Nor did he know the stab these words made into Lamb's heart.

So now here was Lamb and here she was talking to the last person she could ever have imagined she could face again, being a shamed woman and the mother of an illegitimate child. The bomb of her life began to explode.

Even so, when she saw Michael now as she had not seen him in the cruel intervening days, memories raced back to the days when she had had the childish thought that love could never die.

There had been a time not so long before - in her last girlish year - when she would have wished to be in his presence- but not now. That time had been when life was young, a springtime, when the spring promised it would be forever green. Then there was no tree which was not budding, no bird which did not sing and no flower that did not bloom. And the land beckoned to them - Michael and Lamb - with a pledge that their dreams would come true. Nothing they did was forbidden to them. The sun kept them warm and the secret place, forbidden to the world, where the Wild Bull lived, was their inheritance. That time had passed.

Now that world had been brought to an end. The green world was now white and starkly real. These two who had shared a dream now were wracked in its recollection. And this child who was the embodiment of that dream was lost in the woods, the very woods where the dream had seemed so real. Would the child, too, die, as had their dream?

How could God have given them to dream and love?

Was the tragedy of the loss of the boy the end that their loving would be brought to?

How could they have known, Michael and Lamb, that a winter of their souls might come? - that Lamb might came to shame, Michael to despair, the Wild Bull to the mark of one hunted to be killed.

The strain of confronting Michael himself was almost more than she could bear. Could she not have been forewarned by some angel not to come home this Christmas? Could not this same angel have warned her not to taste of the fruits of the Garden of Eden? No such warning angel had come to her to intrude into the garden.

She had thought to take the wrath of the world upon herself. She would never have consented to drag Michael down to the depths of her fallen state. Must all of the dismal truth of her life now be brought out? Love, how the torment does not end! Why would the universe not stop its trumpeting!

Reality struck back into the scene. She must look to the moment! Lemuel's notice that her son was lost came back to mind and broke the spell of the surprise of Michael's presence. Lemuel was tearfully talking with her. "Pleasant slipped away from me hours ago while I was supposed to be watching him. His whereabouts cannot be discovered but his tracks led down by the barn, down the hill to the crick behind the barn, and perhaps toward Blue River. I felt pressed to have the posse help with the search for the boy."

There was nothing that might hold back Lamb's terror. Her shrieks and cries rent the air and alarmed all of nature. She did not stand to talk further, but ran off toward the barn and beyond, toward the woods she knew so well, where Michael caught up with her as she slipped in the snow beyond the gate into the back barn lot. By now her screams were muffled by her heavy breathing. Reaching for her, Michael would help her arise but could not help but melt at seeing Lamb's eyes for their tears were turning her face into something horrifying to see. The ice of the air turned both of their breaths into pluming gusts.

Michael said, "Lamb if you will, Let me go with you to reclaim our son."

At the revelation that he knew, Lamb no longer sought to rise but just sank back to the ground and into the snow. What further disaster could now clutch at her throat? Now she must be hated by the only man she had ever loved. Now she must reveal how careless she had been in their love and how hopelessly scandalous a person she had become, filled with such shame that even her mother had died rather than live in its reality.

But Michael would not allow her to lie there in the snow. Holding her up to himself, he would warm her wordlessly in his arms until her composure returned.

"We cannot think of ourselves right now," Michael said. "We must go find the boy. Heaven will give us the strength."

The other men of the posse had ridden their horses on ahead while Michael, their leader, had stayed behind to gain further information. The men of the posse had found the tracks in the snow which led further down the crick where lay a sand bed bearing the child's footprints which then led back to the place where the crick makes a rush through some heavy rocks. They passed through craggy narrows beneath a high bank of mud swelling down from a hill crest.

But here was a stranger discovery yet! In the confusion of the footprints those of the Wild Bull had been discovered at the border crick fence with the next farm south. It was obvious that the little boy had climbed over the border crick fence but he had apparently been joined by another guest of the scene, one which caused the men of the posse to cock their guns. Gusts of snow were falling in sheets. No creature, unhoused or sheltered, would make it through this perilous day.

Then they picked up the trail where the crick opened out into horse pasture. The boy had followed the banks of the crick down this pasture. Up ahead they heard the laps of the more powerful Blue River and, with eyes sweeping back and forth across the terrain, they observed the river itself. Its sound was the trilling triumph of a powerful flow. Full strength watery blood coursed the vein.

Back at the farm, Michael and Lamb were aroused. They heard shots blasting into the air from far down the crick toward Blue River.

"It is the posse," Michael said. He looked down in the direction of the shots. "Some of those who have gone ahead must have run into some danger. The boys of the posse came upon the call by your father that his grandson was lost in the treacherous woods this icy day." And yet the shots were not only fired in sound far away. To Lamb it might have been a shot fired at her heart. What if her son were injured?

There was no stopping them from doing what they felt compelled to do. The two ran breathlessly in great strides down the hillside from the huge barn splashing their way over the ford at the otherwise icy breadth. Through the meadow too they rushed, heedless of the huge rocks washed up by the raging spring turbulences and limbs and holes. They moved down into the river's next mile, The woods beneath the ancient trees was clear of brush and they could move quickly toward the sound of the shots along this section of the Blue River banks. Far up ahead was the source of the shots, into the Blue River wilds where Dilly Crick emptied.

And then after time passed so slowly, when they could draw the scene into recognition, they could see the men of the posse in a semicircle around an object caught between them and the line of Blue River.

The woods was at its deepest here. The boles of the trees were of the thicknesses of many people and their ridged barks seemed as vertical support for few limbs at all until reaching perhaps 200 feet in the air where the limbs exploded into dark and leafless branches.

The posse had been taken completely by surprise. The Wild Bull of Blue River lay resting before them.

Desperate thoughts ran through the posse's minds.

How could this have been? The Wild Bull snuck up on! Impossible. It could never happen. Was this a mirage appearing from winds too wild? Never in the past years had the Bull allowed itself to be discovered in any position of vulnerability.

The Wild Bull would have heard them coming for miles. They all knew this intuitively and worry and anxiety kept them frozen in their tracks while stinging arrows of doubt pierced them.

However it had happened, caught along the river near its course under the bridge called the Great Iron Lady of Blue River was the Wild Bull of Blue River. Close by was another object they now recognized as the boy. The little boy was resting its head upon the beast's flank and strangely the Wild Bull would not move even at the instance of the continuing shots aimed over him and designed to scare him into moving away from his position between the boy and the river. The Wild Bull was holding his ground sheltering this child and offering its own flesh as a barrier between the boy and the icy river, even though it might mean its death. It was clear from the tracings that the bull had walked between the child and the river for a mighty distance and then there had been some inexplicable commotion evidenced at the river. Now the bull and boy were before them.

"Hold on! He has the child at his mane," one of the posse members shouted to halt the group from immediately killing the hated beast.

To the most accurate marksman and sharpshooter of the posse, Thomas Lineback, the instruction was given to climb to the bridge nearby and prepare a shot to kill the Wild Bull at the first opportunity for clear targeting and firing. Soon Thomas scrambled up to the bridge with his rifle. He took a position in clear sight of the bull and the boy. Thomas had the reputation for being the quickest and straightest shooting gunman of them all. He also was said to have the least compunction about using his weapon. His theory was to drill his target, whether horse thief or burglar, through the center of the head which is messy but finishes off the problem with certainty. "No good nicking a man or shooting him in the leg," he would say. "The fellow will just do it again." He had in fact killed one rustler in Hancock County and another just across the county line into Rush.

How could this friendly bridge, the Great Iron Lady of Blue River, countenance a person brandishing a gun? She was built to span, to mediate, to offer passage. She was the summit and very mark of Hoosier ingenuity, determination and industry. Her trussing panels were wide to offer crossers the safest passage and her top chords were angled variously to turn her into the most beautiful bridge in all the world -everyone said so. And yet upon her soon stood a posse member whose rifle, carefully aimed, would seek the Wild Bull as its sure target at his earliest opportunity.

The other members of the posse could do no more than await the events unfolding. Only an occasional shot fired over the Bull's head could be tried to move him from his horrible proximity to the defenseless child. Some wondered if the child was even alive! Had the bull killed the boy and stayed there with him as his trophy, its taunt to the world about its already acknowledged horror?

No member of the posse was brave enough to approach the Wild Bull to snatch the boy from the clutch of this storied monster.

The Wild Bull would only rear his massive head at the shots and dare the posse men to leave him to his task of safeguarding this child from death.

Arriving at a pant, Lamb saw Pleasant at once. There he was, the little boy on a bank leveling into a sand bar near the dangerous depths of Blue River. She also noted how the boy was obstructed from encountering the river by the Wild Bull who lay sheltering him with his bulk. There was no taunting or defiance about the bull. More ominous would have seemed the sycamores and corkscrew willows whipping the frothing river with their branches during this wild windy blizzard.

Then at a run, Lamb rushed to the little boy to take him to her breast to warm and revive the frozen child. As Lamb took the boy to arm to warm him up, she noted with horror, "He has been wet." She turned to Michael in despair. "This child has fallen into the river for his clothes are freezing." She threw off her own coat to cover the boy and quickly removed his frozen garments.

"Michael, his clothes!" Lamb shouted. "He has not only been wet, but his coat bears a rip where it has caught on something!" Michael began assisting Lamb in rubbing the boy back to warmth after pulling off his wet and icy clothes. Soon a blanket was brought to her by one of the posse members from his horse.

In the instant all of this was taking place, Michael looked at the creek. Yes, Michael could clearly see where there had been ice broken in the crick, huge sections of it, far larger than a boy could make, had been slashed through. There was no person close to have gashed such a passage through the ice to the shore. The break in the ice was apparent even in the heavily falling snow. Michael looked at the Wild Bull in bafflement.

Lamb looked at Michael in equal query. "How could the boy have gotten out of the river if he had fallen in?" she asked. The question could only remain unanswered.

Only then did Lamb glance at the Wild Bull still, in the seconds that had passed, at his rest where he had been.

"His horn!" she shouted. "Michael, look at the Wild Bull's horn."

A few simple but clearly recognizable shreds of the boy's coat were wrapped tightly around the Wild Bull's horn during his rescue of the boy. "Michael," Lamb said, "the Wild Bull has pulled the boy from the river by the coat and using his horn!

Michael too was shaking his head in wonder. "Lamb," he said in relief, "I believe that Wild Bull played 'Gore and fetch' with our son and pulled him out to safety."

But the day's activities were not at an end. Far from it.

Shortly after Lamb carried the boy away from the Wild Bull, the marksman, Thomas Lineback, saw his chance. He had awaited a moment to empty his rifle's load into the Wild Bull. He had been standing at the ready on the nearby bridge, The Great Iron Lady of Blue River. If any might succeed, it would be he. His was the reputation for being the fastest and straightest shooter of the posse. Before him was an unobstructed target in the beast that had not ever been available to a person ever before. Here was the chance of a lifetime to kill the Wild Bull.

Raising his rifle to dead level Thomas took aim and began a deadly dispatch into the unsuspecting and helplessly targeted Wild Bull of Blue River, but somehow an imperfectly and hastily aimed shot missing the head, and instead ringing into the bull's flesh.

Was the Wild Bull wounded or dead from this blast?

A burning icy meteor struck the Wild Bull in the flank and blood began its ooze out from the proud beast. The shot had exploded into the beast's thigh as a tornado rips down and destroys. All the posse, flushed with the unexpected initial success, concentrated their aims again, this time with every intent to finish the job and kill the beast that endangered the little boy so decidedly and had for so long terrorized the land.

Billowing blood flows began their streams down the wounded bull's flank and yet he did not stand to run. He merely looked up at his attackers as if in wonder. Escape was impossible for him anyway. He would accept that he must die. He would accept that his task of life was at an end. Perhaps someday Lamb might think of him and that would be sufficient to justify his life. He had repaid his mistress for his own life by saving her son on these selfsame banks where she had saved him as a calf so many years ago. His wound must prove fatal except that help be obtained.

Thomas Lineback, swearing for missing the kill, took aim to shoot again and this time not to miss the head.

"Hold your fire," one of the rescuers said. Thomas eased his finger from the trigger. "What is going on," he yelled back.

The scene was this. When Lamb had heard the ring of the shot, the look in her eye was as an angry sword. Then she had reacted to the shot instinctively, rushing to the aid of the Wild Bull so that the target could no longer be pursued without danger to her and her son. Lamb had seen what none of the others had seen. The Wild Bull had saved her child from an icy grave.

She did not merely throw herself in harm's way. Lamb also, even awkwardly holding her child, gave the Wild Bull such hugs for saving Pleasant that the bull must have known how comforting would be the ministering angels themselves to those undergoing final pain.

"Just hold off," one shouted up to Thomas Lineback, "The mother has run at the Wild Bull on some account. We might hit the mother." In the confusion and tumult, the posse members waited, guns raised, fearful of what next might follow. It was clear to them all that danger still lurked. The Wild Bull was still terrible.

He roared from the wounds and his body was shaking into contortion. He involuntarily shook off Lamb's embrace and raised up his bulk as if to try to move one last time but fell limply down, bellowing in pain, his back leg useless for running, and restrained by the force of a shot from rising. His only movement was coming from waving his head in agony.

The Wild Bull had hardly had time to look to his unknown attacker from where he had been on the watch for the little boy to keep him from coming closer to the icy waters of Blue River before his own blood was pouring out as if the Bull had only been a sack ready to be rent of his red contents all these days.

But Lamb could not be restrained from staying with the Wild Bull and between the wounded bull and his attackers. Finally through the horrible aching from the pain, the Bull took notice that his beloved Lamb was by his side and the worst of his threshing came under control. He would not endanger his mistress.

Michael could only shout, "Hold your fire," as the men did as bid undertaking no further engagement in the business. "It's over boys," Michael shouted. "The child has been found and is safe. We have done our job and we can return to our homes."

Perplexed but obedient, the posse began its retreat from the Christmas scene. Lamb left the Wild Bull and went to attend to Pleasant further. "Let my son's life be fully restored," began her repetitive and continuing prayer until she was convinced by his more attentive look that Pleasant was recovering. She would hold him closely to herself, finding him cold but warming him within her coat until the sleepy eyes would open, there beside the dying Wild Bull, and she knew that all would be well with the child.

Then Lamb, seeing the Wild Bull so wounded, returned to the Bull, her Prince, in a pool of his pouring blood, handing the boy to the closely observing father. Tears from her eyes joined the surging blood of the bull poured out for the saving of her child.

For the first time, Michael held the child he had never known of. The sight of the father united at long last with a child unknown was an appearance as trumpets sounding in Zion. Michael recognized the boy immediately. It was the very boy, the vulnerable child, he had rescued from the Gypsies. He knew it from the minute he saw the boy's eyes. The boy had Lamb's eyes. Here were those same eyes that had haunted him and set his mind to whirling. Here was the child who would reshape his life and turn him into a father.

Michael, now holding his child, joined Lamb, and the boy and the dying Wild Bull. He prayed that his spirit might be steadied.

By this time, Lemuel had arrived, and though he was shocked to see his daughter so near the wounded bull he heeded Michael's request that he leave them, the three of them, to the scene. The remnants of the posse left on the promise of Lemuel to provide them all with a bracing malty beer in his warm kitchen before they should return to their homes for the rest of the Christmas Day.

Michael handed the child back to the mother, removed his shirt, damned the weather, and bandaged the bleeding bull's wounds. These injuries turned the impromptu bandages scarlet. Would they stop the stricken bull from bleeding to death? When no more could be done, Lamb brushed off the snow from Michael's overcoat and helped Michael on with it clutching at her son all the while.

The piling snow might prove the bull's death. He must be taken to the barn and yet how might this occur? The bull was severely weakened by malnutrition as well as suffering horribly from the wound with his bloodletting.

"Oh Wild Bull," she said, "Oh Wild Bull," she cried out to the wind.

She bowed her head to her wounded pet's flank and the Bull turned in his agony to see her. How he had missed her. How he would prance for her even now if he could. How he would give to her every nudge of his love.

"Wild Bull, you cannot survive down here in this condition," she told her pet. "You must rise up and come with me back to the barn."

But the Wild Bull's eyes were blearing and his head drooped back to the ground. With her hand she brushed his flank and took her hand back to where the wound was bloodying the rag made from Michael's shirt.

"Oh, Wild Bull, I will not allow you to die!" Lamb said.

She rose from her bending and lifted up his head and looked into his eyes, "Come my Prince." "Stand up my Prince and let me lead you to the barn and recovery!" With each breath, in the presence of his lifegiver, Lamb, the bull breathed more confidently and thickly. For her, he would live. Wouldn't now the days of estrangement be over? He remembered being the weaning calf in Lamb's lap. He recalled memories that cast defiance at his injury. They were recollections that lifted him and began carrying him through the pain.

The Wounded Bull focused his blearing eyes. The little girl of his dancing days of youth was pleading with him. His body shook in the wracking pain.

Lamb tugged at his head, "Please, Wild Bull, arise. Go with me!" She was begging and crying. "You must not die here. You are my only proof that love cannot die!"

The head so limply bemoaning shook and shook and his flank with it, his tail falling in place, while his shoulders took a momentous push forward which lifted his body as the Wild Bull of Blue River arose and trailing behind his mistress and followed by his trailing of blood, he would take the steps of pain which would slowly allow his dragging body to come to the crick and then ford its passage and follow his mistress, however strange might be her mission, wherever she might lead him.

He would try now to live to engage the experience of this reunion. The eyes of the bull, borne on great pouches, peacefully were eyes that had only and ever been focused for this long awaited reunion. Life had returned to him his angel after all these months, the warming presence who he had thought would not be seen ever again, long anticipated, the spring in every romp.

Into the barn and a horse stall aside its main floor entry, Lamb betook the Wild Bull of Blue River. And now the three, Michael, carrying his son, and Lamb would stay beside the limping bull in the barn of warmth and safety. Soon the Wild Bull was bedded down, watered and fed of the corn and hay of Lamb's father's storing.

Here was the bed of the Wild Bull and here Lamb and Michael would stay for yet awhile with Pleasant close beside. They would join with the Wild Bull and encourage him to make his stand for life.

No longer would the Wild Bull need to awake into a world that hated him and hunted him and shot at him at every turn, and where his one consolation was only an expectation, never a certainty, that sometime there would return, in person and not merely in his dreams, the hand of the gentle child who had bottle fed him in his hunger when he should have died for lack of a mother's milk.

Now the Wild Bull whose gamey shattered thigh made dangerous rushes a thing of the past, had a reason to rest.

Then with the scene that of peace, Lamb could look up at Michael saying to him. "Oh, Michael, I am so happy to see you again. I am so glad to see the happiness in your eyes. I am so glad to see you happy as you are even in this dismal scene. It must be true. You are now in love. The happiness your face shows must reflect a passion from your heart."

"Yes," Michael said. "It is true Lamb I am in love." Then he bent down to look at her. "Lamb I am in love with no one but you. I have always been in love with you. There is no room in my heart for any other. There never has been."

How strange it was for Lamb to learn that, despite her fallen state, she was loveable? So strange to hear this news in the circumstances and in the presence of her wounded Wild Bull. She responded from all her heart. "And I, Michael, I was not born except to love you. I would die rather than hurt you with me as a burden you might not wish, or my child be an obligation you would not know, or want, to have. Oh, Michael," she said grasping for the right words..."And then, at my return from town and up at the barn, when I learned that Pleasant was lost, I was afraid it was all over, my life and the life of the child - our child."

Michael shook his head in frustration! "You should have given me the opportunity to continue to love you, Lamb. You know that is all I have ever wanted to do in my life. Instead I could only wander from place to place, tormented and deluded into seeing you everywhere except never close, dreaming of you day and night."

Michael looked down at the little one in his arms. "And is this child truly the product of our love?" he asked.

"He is yours, Michael," Lamb said simply. "His name is Pleasant." "Forgive me, forgive me, Michael," Lamb asked. "Forgive me if I have caused you heartache. Please just hold me in your arms."

"Oh, Lamb, I was so afraid I would never see you again. I could not bear it if you went away again. I could not rid you from my mind or my life. Tell me you will stay beside me forever. You must never leave me again. Our love can never be over," Michael told her. "Won't you marry me?"

"Oh yes, yes!" she said.

And the Wild Bull of Blue River looked up from his agony to see Michael and Lamb in an embrace, made a little cumbersome by a little boy insisting on joining into it.

"Say do you hear music?" Michael said coming up for air. "Pinch me," Lamb said,"that I might know I am not asleep. Yes, Michael you are the same man." Then she asked, "Michael am I the same girl I used to be?"

"Oh, Yes," Michael said.

And down where the sounds were of rills would run the crick into Blue River, the little river that trickled and beckoned the land to respond to life's presence. It was a witness of everything that God did in the country, along with the huge towering sycamores and short, shaking corkscrew willows that bent their branches into the waters. Here was the same river of their youth and its spring when the river sheltered the banded water snakes both in its branches and where they touched the flowing river water, permitting them to strike into its waves and extract an occasional minnow swimming by.

The river's song of the moment was encouragement for the wandering of the world to come to its banks.

And later, Michael and Lamb, after taking Pleasant inside to the arms of her father for watching, would walk to the Blue River along whose course were moss covered stones visible between the icy floes stopping the gravely and sandy beds from eroding downstream and carriage away. The blizzard was over and now there fell a glow of a wintry night, and even an occasional breaking through of starlight pierced the scene.

Then the icy Blue River began to sing another song.

"Come to me for your every Passover," it lapped, remembering in its flowing the sting of every hurt and even the former dilemma of the little boy who would now grow in the company of an attending pet, a Wild Bull. The future was for them.

Michael and Lamb studied each other in silence for the longest while, every glance ripping away an interval of the time of separation, and then he had looked at her more directly.

He had taken her hand.

There was now certainty where before had been doubt. The certainty was that of one who said, "Are you only a visitor to Jerusalem and do not know the things that have happened there in these days?"

And then they had walked down the bank further.

The even places saw Michael draw Lamb nearer to him.

And then when they could feel the story of their lives burn toward each other and they could not allow the moments of the burning to avoid breaking out, they stopped and approached a rock, flushed of its snow.

Michael sat down on the rock, and looked into Lamb's eyes. And Lamb looked too into his eyes.

"It is true," she said, "love never dies."

18

Hoosier Wedding Day

Lamb insisted, "We shall have our wedding in the barn where our bull recovers in his stabling."

For the Wedding Day, the neighborhood threshing crew had volunteered to prepare the barn and its cavernous threshing floor area and vicinity, and had done so with the same energy they had in cleaning up a field of its wheatheads. Soon the barn's ground floor was emptied of its crude machines, hames, collars, bridles and wagons, swept out and aired. A huge Christmas wreath of evergreen was hung over the barn door and Christmas trees lined the scheier-brick or stone banking leading to the entry.

So now, only three days later, the neighbors were arriving back the long lane to the Hackleman home for the wedding. Their invitations had come by word of mouth, neighbors passing along the glad tidings that Michael Sipe and Lamb Hackleman, so long apart, were to be married. Surprisingly fast flew the news of the wedding, passing as if with the wind, or as fire spreads on a weedy field to be cleared for planting. The news engulfed the neighborhood. Everyone learned of the event and planned to attend. Even John Pritchard, the indefatigable buyer of straw for the paper mill, heard of it and decided to attend. He could snoop around Lemuel's place a little and find out if there might be some more straw there to strike a deal on. The news was as joyously widespread as if the bright yellow field canaries had lifted themselves from the seedy Canadian thistles of summer to broadcast the news across the croplands.

It's time for the wedding without any delay. Christmas gave the promise of this day but now is the day for the marriage of Lamb and

Michael. Then as the guests arrived the members of the posse, Michael's friends and the brave protectors of the neighborhood, ushered them all. Here the folk of the world came by carriage, buggies and horses. All were showed the way back to the barn marked by silver and golden ribbons, a walk which was carpeted with straw and lined by boughs of evergreen.

Outside the barn was the huge generatormobile of Liberty Trees. The oddly effective contraption was connected with wiring to the inside where the inventor's electric heaters had turned the temperature inside the barn into a rosy warmth. On its wagon seat was Liberty Trees himself, pedaling furiously, wearing his huge greatcoat.

Inside were the wagon loads of pews which the posse members had borrowed from the Gilboa Church. But make no mistake, the appearance of this barn was not as a church. It was as a Christmas fantasyland. Huge wreaths of every evergreen festooned the Deutsch barn's lofts and entries, with Christmas trees tied in red and green bows surrounding the huge interior. All of the evergreens scented the air and made the place seem as outside in a sheltering Christmas tree forest. Candles in every corner and wayside lit the scene.

See the beautiful ladies as they arrive! Their dresses are simple and amazingly alike, straight and flat in front, gored and pleated at the sides and back. But the materials differ. Here is a dress of natural wool. There muslin. There silk. Each bears a decorative and personal touch, a band of lace, colored ribbons, prettily trimmed petticoats with silk trim visible as they move. The top of their sleeves are so fluffy and enlarged making their shoulders have such long horizontal lines! Some wear hats with veils while others wear their hair in the fashionable Greek styles. All seem so different and yet the same, cheerful to be in the select presence of others. All the women seem so much more dressy than their husbands in their frock coats and top hats, giving square shouldered and straight waisted silhouettes. What an affair! This event must be the highlight of the very lives of those of the backlands of the Blue River country!

Whom do we see at the gathering? Not just the farm neighbors and toilers but special ones too. Here the folk of Oklahoma and the Ferrees. There the beautiful mill girls, dressed more plainly in skirts and ties with long waistcoats to keep them warm from the winter weather and with long colored ribbons floating down their backs. They did not mind at all that the mill had been closed by the blizzard these last three days and out of some well of charity, the Greenfield Paper Mill had paid them anyway! So careful they have been of their appearances! One's hair has a short bang and the rest fluffily knotted. Another's hair is drawn to the back and its ends curled. Here is one wearing a ribbon in front, too, where her hair has been crimped on a large iron. How much sweeter smells this barn than the digester building with its odor of caustic soda black liquor! Even Gustavus Crider, Lamb's mill supervisor, has arrived in a great huff. Coming too, and taking places with the mill girls and Gustavus Crider, their supervisor, came Mr. W.H.H. Rock, the stockholder and owner's representative of the Weston Paper Manufacturing Co. itself. He, in his frock coat with shiny patent leather shoes protected by spats, and his lady, Ellis, stylishly slim-waisted and wearing a huge brimmed hat with every imaginable flower and feather, would join as equals in the thrill of the ceremony with the rest and others from the mill and Oklahoma and the farms. What a relief to him to be beyond the call of his stockholders! Now, while Mr. W.H.H. Rock was settled down waiting for the wedding, he suddenly conjured up a question that had been bothering him - How had his riding horse gotten so lathered up a couple of months before? The young handsome men of the posse arrive inside and take their places. The unmarried ones are sneaking peeks at the beautiful mill girls.

The little air-pump organ from the Gilboa church begins its music. It is operated by a bellows expanded by a pedal from the lower casing that is pushed in and out. The organist is a huge woman from a farm on a not too distant ridge. She huffs and puffs. The veil of her hat drawn in under her chin by a string flutters with the heavy gusts of her breath. Do not bust your corset, ma'am, or whalebone will be flying everywhere! The music of Lohengrin emerges from her organ played as mightily as the heavy German woman can make it pressing the pedals in her heavy boots.

At the front of the gathering is an altar festooned with evergreen, huge ties of red ribbons and golden bells.

Michael Sipe takes his place to the front of the altar and Brother Aultman joins him behind the altar with his bible opened. You look so serious, Michael. Smile now at this gathering of friends, will you? His frock coat does not hide the expansive chest heaving so mightily. Now you wear the clothing of a man instead of the knickerbockers with patches and flap pockets which so many of the neighborhood witnesses remember you wearing as a child.

And here comes Lamb Hackleman, alone, down the aisle between the rows of pews in the barn. Lamb you are beautiful in your white dress. You found it, didn't you? You found the dress which your mother, Anna, had made for you after she had banned you from the home, making it from all of the wedding dresses of the Hackleman ladies of the past whose wedding dresses she had come to possess. She had made it for you, her daughter, so lovely and pure!

The silk organza dress is floor length and Anna has hand-beaded it for you. What she could not alter did not need alteration anyway. Her prayers had told her this day would someday come. This dress has been fitted for you by the generations of Hackleman women whose stitching, and trimming in Venise pearled lace survived even the homeless wandering of your ancestors from Germany. You look so beautiful in the lace made of a heavy cotton needlepointed kind in a floral design emblazoned with buttonhole stitching, in the manner of the ancient designs of the City of Mark, Venice. The sleeves are notched above the elbow, free to carry a spray bouquet of poinsettia, holly and ivy. On her head is a silver headpiece, an heirloom from the Palatinate past, from which a blusher veil is suspended.

Lamb's footsteps drew closer to the altar. The crowd quiets as turning they saw her coming from the rear of the barn.

As she passed the front row, she stopped to bend over and plant a kiss on the smiling face of her father, Lemuel Hackleman, sitting on the front row in a seat of honor. The place next to him, where Anna might have sat on another such occasion under other and more favorable circumstances, had been left empty.

And now Lamb proceeded on to arrive to stand beside Michael to take the vows which would mean that she might spend the rest of her life with this man. The days of separation of her life had ended. Facing the pettiness of life had given her wisdom and strength. Having felt so intimately the forces of life, she understood and could now live in the hidden things that occur when love comes close.

Where before, bits of conversation could be picked out amidst the buzz of the crowd, now there descended on the group a silence, an expectation that the mystical event of a union in family was unfolding. The music ceased.

The barn quieted.

Clearing his voice, Brother Aultman began,

"Please be seated."

When the friendly crowd had seated themselves

in the uncomfortable wooden pews, he continued.

"It was an early Christian practice to recall that our lives are lived in the midst of a cloud of witnesses of those who have gone before. Let us remember those who are departed present with us in the sky and the winds and our thoughts and let us bring to this gathering as witnesses from the clouds, the Christian saints and all those flying in the air who are in the family of God.

Shall we pray the prayer of Mark, the Evangelist, who wrote an invocation for the presence of the quick and the dead for his martyred Alexandrian church. Please, shall we pray,"

The congregation bowed their heads in prayer.

"One over all, Jesus Agapa, God who once came to us on earth, Our Familyhead, the one who jointly listens to the story of our lives with the Parent of life and the spirit of the world, great ultimate priest, the bread that sustains us raining down out of reality, and bearing with us the weight of the troubling times in our lives, the one who wards off our vulnerable weaknesses hanging as possibilities in our lives. We bind ourselves to you and we call upon you, our Familyhead, friendly humanity sensitizer, to recall before our faces the love of the quick and the dead to these your children whose marriage permits them to share the world as partner inheritors. Give them, those who are in the clouds as witnesses to the way God attends to the world, to be present with us this day, interceding into this ceremony with a love that transcends time. Amen."

Quietly, so quietly, without notice from the crowd, or anyone, time had parted its curtain, and into the room and taking her seat quietly beside Lemuel came the dead Anna Hackleman, silently as light, Anna, the dead mother of the bride, and companion from beyond of these events, the tired little dead woman who had wished for a relief such as this moment from the time she had known of her daughter's unwed pregnancy. Anna comes out of the place beyond darkness, the homeland which resists the night, the beat of her broken heart only a faded memory that gently and slowly was sealed away with a death enfolding her in its mystery. She appeared in soul, heart, strength and mind to take her place beside her husband. Anna has come home for you Lamb to be with you on this happy occasion, filled with love as angels love, slipping down through the Hoosier winter sky in its white moments of cold freshly touched by the healing hand of dark death. Now, too late, Lamb, you are in the presence of a mother who could not live the lie of the untruth of events. "I have not been cast aside, Lamb," she whispered to her daughter. "My spirit has been freed and I have been forgiven the evil done against you, my own pride in judging you too harshly, before your very eyes." Anna had thought more of the Hackleman family reputation, and how it would be ruined by Lamb's unwed pregnancy, than she had of her daughter. Anna had worn false family pride as a coat against raging weather. Anna now smiles tenderly upon her daughter in freedom that knows no burden of breath, no judging on the basis of whispers of others. She has shed the bitter coat that had made her life so uncomfortable and unliveable.

God, in God's wisdom has decreed it - that this wedding be witnessed by the mother who had wished for her daughter to be reputable every day in her mortal life until, heart broken, she could no longer observe it with physicality. The justification had come in the fullness of time itself.

And when the revitalized Anna reappeared to witness the events she found herself observing the rapture of her daughter about to be married. Somehow, somehow, her daughter had been carried into a situation of family love with a young man, not through the exercize of her damning ban, but by events beyond the control of any hand.

The congregation raised their eyes from their penitency as the service continued.

Strangely to Lamb, upon hearing the prayer, a great relief came upon her. She sensed her disapproving mother to be present in the congregation in a way beyond the comprehension that mortals bear, to have been summoned to be present with her daughter as before, and to appear not in disapproval but in content. And more importantly she now heard in her soul her mother saying to her, "Now you can come home. Your journey has brought you to Jerusalem. Now your home may be founded."

The minister proclaimed the purpose of the gathering.

"Michael Sipe and Lamb Hackleman are here today to be married. I welcome you all, the father of the bride, Lemuel Hackleman, relatives, neighbors, friends, all of you.

There is a purpose to this gatherin'.

Where were we when this moment arose?"

The minister rubbed his head.

"We were all being ourselves when this strange thing happened. Michael and Lamb found each other in a strange way beyond relating after many months of separation, and informed us they wanted to marry. So Michael and Lamb are here to become two selves united into one."

The minister had been addressing the congregation generally.

He then turned to the bride and groom, and asked, "And who gives this woman to this man?" It was the tradition here for the father to say, "Her mother and I."

But Lemuel, Lamb's father, did not arise from his seat. Lemuel had already told Lamb that he could not, in good conscience, give her away since he had known her abandoned from his home and left without the comfort of a parent. Apparently Lamb had failed to inform the preacher of her father's decision. Now that the preacher had asked the question however, might Lemuel arise to avoid the lapse in the ceremony? No, Lemuel could not. Nor could he change his mind even to avoid an awkward moment in his daughter's wedding. His eyes were downcast.

And yet the minister awaited.

The silence hung over the audience.

It was, however, toward the back of the barn that the opening of the huge doors into a back horse stall could be heard. These doors now swung accessible, free of latch, in some quirk of breach of the quiet of the occasion.

Soon the noise was too great to ignore and the guests arose to turn to look. A push to the door of the stall by a beast inside had cracked it open. As the squeaking door opened further, a great anguished rustling inside could be heard. The widely cracking door to the stables was open now and within could be heard a huge commotion and strained movement. Inside the Wild Bull of Blue River had painfully aroused himself to his feet. Since there was no one else to come forward for Lamb, the Wild Bull of Blue River would fight off the pain to do so.

Then the Wild Bull noisily drew himself forward despite the wounding of his flank. Now he was outside the stall and could observe all these people in front of him. The ceremony itself was visible to the beast from the stable door he had cracked open. Seeing Lamb and by her side, Michael, he had had no hesitation what to do.

Gimpily as on the wounded leg he walked, he lumbered down the aisle at the wedding.

At the sight of the Wild Bull, a dread which all of the neighborhood knew, the neighbors and friends had arisen from their seats, some with horror. Here was a woman screaming. A man was trying to calm another rushing for the door. The audience moved from the aisles as the Wild Bull limped in his agonized way down the aisle toward the altar. Another man was rushing outside the barn shouting that he would get a gun he kept in his wagon. Another was sheltering the last row of guests seated in the rear with a coat outstretched and which he was waving wildly at the beast. Gustavus Crider pulled a .38 Smith and Wesson from his waistcoat wanting to fire it off but restrained out of fear that an innocent bystander might be hit as well.

Each step was a nightmare requiring more strength than Wild Bull could summon. Some strength from beyond was providing assistance but even that began fading. And the rising turmoil of the guests was not lost on the Wild Bull. Here was even Frank Schlopfhs (rhymes with chops), one of the guests, recognizing him again for possessing the perfect ribeye! That strange glint in the butcher's eyes reappeared and its look was not lost on the Wild Bull. This fellow is going to be after my round steak again, Wild Bull feared.

He turned to see the barn door opened wide. But he would not leave this assembly where Lamb was. He held his peace only halfway to the altar.

Unseen by the world, Anna arose from her seat of observation beside Lemuel. She noted Wild Bull's pain. Anna would go to him and give him comfort. Hadn't she brought him through his worst danger with this Frank fellow at the abattoir once? Now she would encourage him again. Wild Bull felt Anna by his side and gave a little nod to clear his head.

Anna assured him. "Yes, Wild Bull, go to the altar. There is no one I trust more to be with Lamb. We, Lemuel and I, her parents have forfeited our right to stand by her now for failing to stand by her before, but you can go be with her for us. Wild Bull, go to the altar, as wounded by life as you are, to be with Lamb and Michael. Let there be no more separation of those who love each other, ever."

Wild Bull would go to the altar. He could not agree more.

Even as the Wild Bull came forth, he was seen now as he had not been before, ever, in the sight of people. He had lost much of his flesh this winter while he had had no livestocker to feed him and his flank was tucked with hipbones visible straining against the skin.

He was no danger, except the danger of the ambiguity of life itself, whereby what is feared may be no threat, what is perceived may be misinterpretation, what is puissant is weak. And despite it all somehow, love prevails and drives forward life and even stranger it preserves and not just allows life to go on but saves it too from every destruction.

The Wild Bull's task was before him. His eyes were steadfast on Lamb and Michael as the Wild Bull, tired beyond all exertion, would go forward to fall to the feet of the bride. Then, after Wild Bull reached the altar, Lamb felt compelled to speak to the milling folk. Lamb could not allow this moment of peace to turn into one of terror. She quieted the guests with calm voice. "Do not be frightened," she said. "Do you not see he is weighed down with his wounds? Give him peace. Please friends do not cast further abuse or scorn on this beast. He has ever been my pet and he suffered wounding to save a child. He wishes to join Michael and me at the altar and, if he wishes to, Michael and I do as well. He is a hero to us. He could have run away but would not so that a child would not drown in an icy watery grave. His blood flowed until he was pale but no more will he ever languish if I live, for his appearance to me is the brightness of an everlasting spring morning."

And the guests began their return to their seats, eyeing this Wild Bull of Blue River. Had he saved a child? How could the Wild Bull be a saving creature? In fact he now, on closer observation, seemed so vulnerable himself.

The guests watched attentively filled in wonder. The wounded bull would be permitted in their midst, even as he was. They would take Lamb's word that he would render no harm with a rush. And then returning to the altar, the minister recommenced the service.

There had been no need for the question, "Who gives this bride to this groom?"

All understood that the bride was given to the groom by the Wild Bull of Blue River.

The minister resumed the service saying to Michael and Lamb, "You two may now join hands."

They had willingly done so with glance that smiled and carried the recapture of the two in peace with the hour.

"And now you two become one body in the life of God who came to earth, And we give you an explanation of the primacy of family love from Paul's Corinthian correspondence.

Michael and Lamb, you have in you a flood of Hoosier, the scripture to follow is Paul's "Family Love" passage from the Bible in its Hoosier version:

"And still I want to explain to you
something of a more ultimate goal. If I speak
so as to communicate with persons or those
beyond death, but have no conceding family
centered love, I am a brass horn blaring out,
or a cymbal clashing.

And if I have done preaching and I know
the answer to ever puzzle and know everything
and even have faith so's to remove a mountain,
but I don't have a conceding family building
love core, I am nothing.

And if I give pieces of bread as charity
to the last penny I got, and if I give the
clothes off of my back, so as to boast what
good I done, but I don't have family love for
my folk brothers and sisters, I fail myself.
Love is patient. Love is caring. It don't
stir up jealousy, or indulge in brags, or give
any ground for arrogance. It don't rest on
behaving acceptable, or look after its own
interest at all, or lose its even temperament
no matter what happens, or fail to consider
the worst or find happiness in injustice, but
instead finds joy in its own reality.

It endures everything, stays faithful
despite everything, sees hope in everything,
remains steady through everything. This
family centering love never fails.

Whether preaching is heard or not, the sermons lose their sound.

Whether spiritual communication happens or not, it ends.

Whether knowledge comes about or not, it will be rendered out of date. For we know only in bits and we preach only about life pieces.

But when comes end-time maturity, the piece-mealing ends. When I was a baby, I talked as a baby, I behaved as a baby, I understood as a baby. Then I become an adult. I passed through the stage of baby ways. Just so now, we see through a mirror in shaddurs, but then face to face.

Now I only know some, but then I will have knowledge beyond knowing and beyond imagining. In our lifetime, faith, hope and love keep us going, these three. But of the most importance is conceding family building love. Follow after this goal of love, seek after it through spirit engaging activity. It is most apparent through bringing those we are close to a joining into a God approved life."

The minister now became his most solemn self.

"I now ask you to profess vows of your giving of yourselves to each other."

He looked at the two very seriously, eyes squinted in his most solemnly quizzical look.

"Do you two wish to be married?"

Both Michael and Lamb said "Yes" clearly and unequivocally.

"Do you recognize that this state represents an approved lifestyle?"

"Yes", they responded.

"As married persons will you live so as to give no substantial cause for offense to the other and cast no blame on the other which would serve to cleave the bond of marriage.

"Yes," they responded.

"Will you patiently endure with each other everything, in trouble, in duty, in emergency, in sickness, in anger, in work, in anxiety, in life pangs, in avoiding despair, in understanding, in care, in inspiration, in sincere love, in honest words, in the potential God has given to you, over pride or humiliation, through slander or fame?"

"Yes", they again responded.

Satisfied, the old minister now relaxed a moment from delivering his charge to the young ones entering into marriage.

"I now ask you if you have rings to exchange?"

Again they responded in the affirmative.

"You may exchange them."

As they did so he said, "These rings will represent your union. They will set yourselves into a little community of two. Look at them as good times come, hang onto the shared memories of these events. Pain will come, These rings will remind you of the strength you have in your shared vulnerability. Time will go on - end - re-exist, Your rings represent the vows you take today."

Addressing the congregation, Brother Aultman said, "I ask you, all of you, to join with me in a prayer of commitment to the marriage of Lamb and Michael."

"Our God, Here we are. We had thought all this time, and from time to time, that we were living for our own benefits individually and Michael and Lamb are telling us this day otherwise. They tell us just the opposite in a breath that bears the validity of a speech with the truth of the gift of God's life. They tell us that life is to be shared in family love. They recognize their love to each other as well as to the life they share. They reject that life has no worth. Their joint worth, come from their vulnerability for each other, strengthens them with the same strength that holds together atoms and galaxies, the cement that God's will will be done. They together share the joy of life, this joy being a citadel of each other that cannot be torn down. Let them know that they have a Trinity full of encouragers for their union."

Then, his voice arising to a great shout, the minister said,

"Thanks be to God, also the father of our Familyhead, Jesus, God when on Earth, the parent of mercy and God of all encouragement, the one who strengthens us and keeps us safe, so that we are able to withstand all our trouble in doing those things we are called to do, despite affliction, and with the assistance of the Comforter, God's strong right arm, allow them and us to have the bonding feel for us of God on Earth as from God on Earth it abounds and comforts and speeds us. And give them as well a transformation of their lives and the comfort of each other. And give them peace in each other, a deserved peace, based upon a recognition that they live in the life story of Jesus, the God informational principle, and outreach, that bears up them and us, forever and ever, Amen."

At the conclusion of this prayer of commitment of the congregation to their life and the great life principles, the minister then pronounced the marriage.

"And now I, as the bearer of the good news of the life you have chosen to share, announce that you are Husband and Wife."

He then added, "You may greet the congregation as married folk."

The two young people, now husband and wife, turned to face the congregation of relatives, and friends, all well wishers. There was a welling up of good feeling terminating in hands clapping. Cast aside were all feelings of ill, grief, brokenness. Peace prevailed turning everyone's heart who was there to laughing. A bright tide of goodwill burst out which flowed over the congregation and overflowed into the Blue River valley. And the Wild Bull of Blue River felt the peace and arising to stand with this pair and share the joy of the events was also the Wild Bull of Blue River.

Before the congregation stood youth, awakened from sleeping, hands of two which had been unclasped, now joined, clear eyed, now able to observe with sharpened power, a world finally revived, warmed and refreshed.

After the smiles and expressions of joy and the conversations of delight and friendship had abated, Michael raised his hand as if for silence.

The barn full of guests quieted down, and the newly married Lamb announced to the guests, "Please be seated again."

With some surprise the guests returned to their seats and seated themselves.

Michael said, "We have another visitor to join with us on this occasion."

After a moment in which curiosity of the congregation built, Michael added,

"And now I wish a little boy to come to us."

From the back emerged the little boy Pleasant, dressed in the most beautiful white knickerbockers that ever a child had worn. Safely in the magic of the occasion, he had stayed patiently as his mother had directed, to await her cue to be brought into the gathering light. His moments before the wedding, awaiting its triumph, had been quiet in solitude, a hush of innocence awaiting the proof of its value. Peace itself seemed to grow and well over the crick country as he was called forward and every veil of anguish was lifted away irrevocably.

As Pleasant walked toward his beckoner, it was clear that this was the hour of knowing, this was time when the truth was to be found, the future of life itself to be affirmed, as discovered out of time and the night, a "parter" of the world from all alienation and despair, as if his joinder with his parents were a previously hidden key unlocking the heaviest door.

The little boy passed down the aisle of smiling neighbors and friends. This one turned to that one, conversation growing, and suspense building.

The child could not be the source of hurt or puzzling.

Alone, surely, in this holy place, the boy went to his breathlessly awaiting mother, gaining more confidence and smiling more fully with each step, so that the three of them might together grow even in the presence of the Wild Bull of Blue River who had saved this boy's life. When he arrived, Michael and Lamb pulled him to them in a family hug.

The congregation had been surprised. They had known of a wedding of two, not of three! Now had come that additional reunion.

But soon one guest, the first, a particularly perspicacious neighbor, then another, began to clap with appreciation of the event, its meaning obvious, something understood, not requiring explanation. Those who had known of Lamb's strange absence from her parents' farm over the months, who had been touched by the depression of Anna and her tragic death and Michael's gnawing loneliness, though not seeing the events as related, could now see how it could be so, and they responded to the event by rising from their seats and clapping and talking excitedly about the event unfolding in front of them, the reformation of a family from experiences beyond telling.

Lamb Sipe looked up to the congregation confidently and said, "Almost two years ago, a little boy was born. Yes, we shall call this day from here on out to be somebody's birthday, and do you know whose it is?" she asked the little boy embraced in Michael's hug?

"ME!!!" said Pleasant in the loudest talk ever of a child that age.

Michael asked the crowd, "Would you all join us in a Happy Birthday to our little Birthday Boy, who is all of our future and past?"

Anna, dressed in her eternity, looked over at Michael with astonishment. So it was he who had been the father of Lamb's child! How could she have been so blind? Now she understood what her condemnation of her child's unwed pregnancy had kept from her. Too late she realized that there can be no horror in the truth. Too late she realized that only through loving eyes should the truth be sought, not through condemning eyes. Michael would be the finest son she might have ever known. She would support them now, both of them, from within her sphere of light where turns the axis of life itself. And now her daughter was home.

All the lands are at rest and at peace; they break into singing.

Michael raised his boy to his shoulders and he bore the brightest beaming a little boy's face could bear.

And the congregation of God swelled with a chorus of:

"Happy Birthday to You.

Happy Birthday to You.

Happy Birthday, Dear Pleasant,

Happy Birthday to You."

And then the congregation drew together in a knot of each other and them. And the afternoon began its passage into the melding day as the music in the barn sounded long and happy to those parting.

And then they all headed for the Hackleman house for a reception and to resume their lives in Hoosierdom again.

And many a person drank to the fifth cup of blessings out of the joy of that day.

And may you live to see your children's children as has Anna.

And the joy of that day was as the joy of discovery that Indiana was a mountain over an unknown sea and even all of our inhabited places on this globe are as mountains over unrecognizable seas, Zions, Sinais, and on which mountains all peoples may feast on the fat things full of marrow and feast on wine on the lees. And all may say upon that day, Lo, we have loved our God all this day that God might save us, we who have waited, for gladness and rejoicing await us in salvation, for the hand of our Familyhead has rested on these very Hoosier mountains of the beauteousness of America.

And no longer would there need to be fearful talk of a Wild Bull of Blue River.

For thus says the Familyhead:

Sing aloud with gladness for Jacob,

and raise shouts for the chiefs of

the nations;

Proclaim, give praise, and say,

Save, O Familyhead, your people,

the remnant of Israel.

Hear the story of the Familyhead, O Nations,
and declare it in the coastlands far
away:
say, "He who scattered Israel will gather
him, and will keep him as a shepherd a
flock."
For the Familyhead has ransomed Jacob
and has redeemed him from the hands too
strong for him.
They shall come and sing aloud on the height
of Zion,
and they shall be radiant over the
goodliness of the Familyhead,
over the grain, the wine, and the
oil,
and over the young of the flock and
the herd;
Their life shall become like a watered
garden, and they shall never languish
again.
Then shall the young woman rejoice in the
dance and the young men and old shall be
merry,
I will turn their mourning into joy.
I will comfort them, and give them
gladness for sorrow.
I will give the priests their fill of
fatness and my people shall be satisfied
with my bounty.

And have the merriest of Christmases, all you Hoosiers,
whoever you are, and wherever and whenever you may be!!!